Africa in My Soul

Memoir of a Childhood Interrupted

Africa in My Soul

Memoir of a Childhood Interrupted

Cheryl King Duvall, PhD

Copyright

Dedication

To my parents whom I love dearly... for many years I was hurt and angry at you for your calling to the Mission Field which separated our family and dramatically changed the course of each of our lives.

As I have grown and learned about life with my own family, I have learned to understand your dedication to your values, to God, and to the sacrifices you made.

Dad, I miss you so much and still relish in being your little Pixie. Mom, you are the strongest woman I have known, and no doubt I got my endurance and strong will from you, and I am thankful for the loving relationship we have developed over the past decade.

Neither I nor my brother and sisters were *called* to be missionaries, but I respect the dedication and values you instilled upon us, and can say that it made us all who we are—strong, independent individuals that share a deep love for our families, each other, and you.

And last, I want to dedicate this to all the mothers and fathers and sons and daughters who may feel pain or anger that keeps them from speaking of, or sharing openly, the deep love or hurt and anger they really feel inside. If this, in any way, sounds like you, I pray with all my heart that you will contact your family members and tell them how much you care for them and love them, and begin the healing process.

Cheryl King Duvall, Author

Table of Contents

Map of Nigeria

A characterization of our life and times in Nigeria

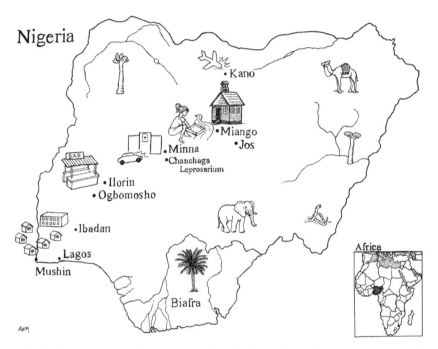

This little map shows the places our family lived the twelve years we were in Nigeria. You can follow our journey from Lagos to Kano. As you can see, we experienced quite a bit of Nigeria.

Aerial View of Kent Academy and Miango Rest Home

The large grouping of buildings in the upper left of the photo is Kent Academy (KA), the boarding school for all missionary kids grades one through nine. The KA chapel (marked with an arrow) is where we went to church. The buildings at the top right are the smaller individual buildings, the teachers' housing. Along the bottom of the photo and under the wing of the plane is the Miango Rest Home where the missionaries take their annual vacations or recuperate from an illness.

Preface

I was born on a Sunday in September in Atlanta, Georgia. According to Mother, I was long, skinny, and downright ugly. Despite a bout with polio at age three and a childhood spent in a culture of strict Christian fundamentalism, I grew strong, determined, partially sane, and ultimately, successful.

It took me several decades to get the nerve to write this memoir. I was concerned about how members of my family and friends would feel about it. I did not want to embarrass anyone in my family. I knew if I wrote my memoir, I would have to speak my truth, and that truth would probably hurt some feelings. It became clear that to free myself, it was time to speak out—not only for myself, but also for my children. I wanted to share my life in Africa with them. It was important for me to share with them the good and the not so good now that they were old enough to understand.

It is also very important for me to share my story with anyone who has a personal dream, a passion, or a "calling." Working towards the achievement of those dreams can be a natural high. I believe one can fulfill those dreams if one works hard enough. But often there are consequences to following your own calling, especially where children are involved. Without setting priorities and recognizing possible outcomes, we often make decisions that have unintended results. Lives may be ruined and families torn apart. God's work may be carried out on the mission field while your own child is being raised and abused by someone you thought you could trust five hundred miles away at your own mission's boarding school for missionary children, or even right on your own mission compound.

My parents were studying at bible college when they made their decision to move to Africa. They were in their early forties in their prime of life. They owned no home of their own. Neither had a stable career, and there were no savings to speak of. They had four children under fifteen, and both of their own families had concerns about them leaving for Africa with their children, not to mention leaving their oldest child of fifteen behind in the states for four years.

In preparation for their new lives, my parents sold all their meager earthly possessions. They left their own parents, brothers and sisters, as well as their fifteen-year-old daughter, and set off for Africa. Shortly after they arrived in Lagos, Nigeria, West Africa, they sent their other three children to boarding school nine months a year for the next decade to be raised by people whom they had initially never met. I won't speak for my younger brother and sister, but I know my parents' decision negatively affected my older sister, and I quickly began to realize just what an impact their decision was having on my life as well.

My parents had been "called" to serve God as Protestant missionaries. They "got the calling" as many missionaries refer to it. Being only ten, as well as an obedient daughter who did not talk back to my parents, I did not have a choice or even a say in the matter. Therefore, I began a life in Africa that was to be both wonderfully exciting and life-changing, yet also filled with loneliness and fragmented by abuse, and some life-shattering experiences. Not your ordinary childhood, to be sure; it was one that I learned at an early age, that I could survive if I fought. Rather than to give in, I preferred to *fight for myself*, sometimes *fighting myself* in the process.

I have been asked many times throughout my life what it was like living in Africa. For those of you who've been there, you know. Africa is magical; the heat is oppressive; the smells are pungent yet stimulating. The colors are brilliant and inspiring, and the people of the land-of-extremes are proud, hard-working, generous, and kind. Never did I meet a person, child or adult, from then until now, who was not in some significant way changed by experiencing life in Africa. As for me, I fell in love with the land and its people, and that love and respect grew throughout the ten years I was privileged to live in Nigeria. It was never Africa or the people who caused me pain. It was the circumstance of being a missionary kid, living within the loneliness and isolation of the missionary compound and the belief system of its fervent followers whose harsh judgement left me with a lifelong pursuit of approval.

I am very passionate in my love for the African people and their country. They are a warm and very hospitable people as I experienced them over the years I lived in Nigeria. Therefore, I want to share some of the experiences my family and I lived through during our decade-plus tenure in many locations throughout Nigeria. But even as I begin to put pen to paper, and in so doing awaken the dragons so tightly locked away in their cages, my chest tightens and the child within me is immediately present. I feel the emotions boiling up, and they will be the force from which you often hear me speak in these writings.

In the process of recalling memories, emotions frequently distort or solidify the so-called facts in your brain. I am sure, in my writings, and as is the case with most people, both have happened. I give you, the reader, the facts as I know and experienced them, when I know or when I think I know them. I will also let you know when I don't know, or don't remember. Some memories are as clear to me as if they had happened yesterday even though they happened in my teens. And some other memories I have blocked, and I can only remember the details around them. This is especially true of some parts of the traumatic events in my life.

For an interesting read on the relationship between memory and trauma, I recommend Peter Levine's book, *Trauma and memory: Brain and Body in Search for the Living Past* (2015). As Levine explains it, the ever-changing eye of the beholder may be the only true reliable defining quality of recollection, and that we cannot observe our memories without changing them in the process of recall. So with that in mind, I promise you my sincerest attempts at authenticity.

Chapter One

Leaving Maria and My Georgia Home

It was a cold, rainy November evening. I felt numb from the strangeness of it all. I still could not grasp what living in Africa would be like, but more importantly, I couldn't understand how we could be leaving my sister, Maria, behind. I knew nothing of the culture shock we would go through in a matter of days. I had never been on a train or airplane. I had barely been out of the country while we lived in Georgia. So instead, Maria's fate consumed my thoughts. I did not know the strange man and woman waiting to take my sister into their home. And I wondered whether they would be kind to her. Would they keep their promise to treat her like their own daughter?

To row: Marie and me.
Second row: Edward and Ann

We stood on the train platform in downtown Atlanta, Georgia, for quite some time, talking amongst ourselves about what was about to unfold. A crowd of people stood next to us, talking and laughing loudly. I felt angry at them for reasons I could not explain. It just felt as if they were intruding on our

1

family gathering that was about to disintegrate. Suddenly, the train that had been quietly parked on the platform where we had been waiting, gave a long, slow hiss. It startled all of us—even our noisy neighbors. The lights on the platform blinked, and there was an announcement over a speaker. I didn't understand anything that was said; nevertheless, my Dad pulled all of us together so that we could collect our belongings.

As we boarded the train, I asked Mother once again why Maria couldn't have come with us, and she replied that it was God's will that she stay in Georgia. I knew I wasn't supposed to argue with God, so that was the end of that. It was evident that Mother was sad. Though she tried to hide them, there were tears in her eyes. I knew Mother tried to be strong and set that Christian example for us, but that often caused her to come across as hard and unfeeling. I had rarely seen her cry. My Dad just kept busying himself with last-minute details. I knew as soon as he got on the train he would break down. I could tell he didn't like this one bit. His family was everything to him.

I remember hugging Maria ever so tightly, and then she was pulled away from me. The train pulled slowly away like a long black slug. The last image I had of my sister was her waving goodbye to us. Strange, I noticed she wasn't crying. I also noticed that my big sister looked so very small.

CLANK...-...clang... clang... CHUG......chug......chug - chug.

As the train hissed and accelerated into the cold blackness, I felt loneliness take a vicious hold of me. I was angry at my parents! I was angry at God! I was even angry at my sister for letting my parents leave her. Surely she could have done something! The loneliness continued until I had to steel myself against it. Numbness enveloped me. The feelings stayed with me, but I let the loneliness and anger blanket me as one would a warm homemade quilt on a cold winter's night. I cleared my mind and closed my eyes tightly, and I found myself drifting, not asleep, but to a different space. I mentally and emotionally "went away," just as I had when Mother harshly punished me, or when I had other feelings with which I couldn't seem to deal.

~ ~ ~

2

The years before we left for Africa, I lived with my family in an older farmhouse in a little town called Stone Mountain, Georgia. Stone Mountain is famous because it has the largest piece of exposed granite in the world. On that large rock mountain is also a famous rock relief, the carving of three Civil War Confederate figures: Stonewall Jackson, Robert E. Lee, and Jefferson Davis—each sitting atop their horses. We often went to the mountain for picnics and to climb the mountain. You could see it in the distance above the tall, southern pines at the back of our land. I lived at that house with Mother, my Dad, my older sister, my younger twin sister and brother, two horses, and a collie named Lady.

The attic to our house had been turned into two small bedrooms, one at each end. I shared a double bed at one end with Maria, my fifteen-year-old sister. She was always hogging the bed, saying that because she was more than twice my age, she needed more than half the bed. I never understood her logic, but I reluctantly moved over. She was always getting the best of me and loved to tease me. On Sunday nights after we got home from church, Mother would usually let us go to bed with a snack. We ate dinner around six p.m. before we went to church, and by the time we came back home and got in bed for the night, it was around nine p.m. For a snack, Mother would give each of us a slice of bread with mayonnaise if we had been good in church. I was always hungry and would eat my bread quickly. But Maria, looking sad and forlorn, would raise her big, beautiful brown eyes and ask me for my last bite.

"NUP, NUP, NOPE! NO WAY! You are not going to trick me into giving you my bread this time!" I'd say through determined teeth. And I meant it!

"But I am twice as big as you are, and I need more to eat to keep me going than you."

Well, I knew that to be true. She could lift a whole bale of hay by herself, and I had to have help. So, I would give her the last bite.

"Oh, Cheryl, this is great! Yours always tastes better than mine. It's wonderful! I am so sorry you will have to watch me eat the rest of mine now! Too bad!" She would then break out laughing, and I knew I had been tricked once again as she pulled her half-eaten piece of bread out from under the covers. She was always teasing me, and I loved the attention she gave me.

My big sister, Maria, was as close to me as a sister could ever be with an age difference of five years. Maria taught me everything I know about horses. I had a Shetland pony, Rusty, and she had a palomino horse, Trigger. In fact, the only reason I got my pony was because she promised my Dad that she would help me take care of her. And she did just that. She had the most loving heart when it came to animals. And that's why, as Rusty got older, I noticed her getting skinny, and she wouldn't run as much as she did in the past, Maria told me that we needed to give her extra love and attention. Maria spared me the real reasons. Rusty was really old and had lost the teeth in the back of her mouth, the ones used for chewing food. There really wasn't anything that could be done for Rusty.

"Yeah, we're going to start feeding her more hay. And you need to brush her twice a day now that school is out. Be very gentle with her. And when Mother isn't looking, bring her a carrot or an apple from the kitchen."

I loved it when Maria brought me in cahoots with her against Mother. It made me feel like I had someone on my side.

The railroad tracks were across the street from our house, and we used to ride our horses, following the tracks for a couple of miles right into town on a Saturday. We had so much fun together on those rides.

"Look out, a train's coming!" Maria would yell.

"Maria, is it true?" I would scream in fright, half in fear, half in happy excitement. And because she would always tease me about a train coming, I never knew when to believe her. She could always do things better than I, especially arm wrestle. When she let me hang out with her, I felt like a big kid. Just being with her made everything all right. Oh, yeah, we argued like normal sisters, but I had a deep love and respect for her. She was my big sister, my friend, my protector against "the enemy." And most times, she didn't even know it.

The other half of the attic was for the twins. Edward and Ann were three years old and had twin beds. Those two were in a world of their own. One of the biggest chores I had was helping to take care of them. Whenever Mother was busy doing something, I would hear her command, "Cheryl, watch the twins." No use in talking back. I knew to follow them around and make sure they didn't get in trouble or hurt themselves. They had gotten fire-engine-red tricycles for Christmas a few months back, and that was all they wanted to do—ride the tricycles on the front tar drive. They were good kids. I actually liked playing with them at times. Both of them were pleasant and easy to get along with for three-year-olds. My little sister had already developed quite an independent nature. Her favorite saying, when she didn't want to be told what to do was, "Please! I do it myself, my way."

My parents came into Maria's and my bedroom one evening as we were beginning to pack our things to move to Africa. The twins had gone to bed. We had already been told we were going to live in Africa so my parents could become missionaries to serve God. At the age of three, it was hard for Edward and Ann to understand what all of that involved. As I recall, they thought we were just moving far away. I envied them because it didn't seem to worry them as it did me. I had too many questions Mother and my Dad hadn't answered. Maria had just as many. We had a lot at stake. What about our friends at school? What would they say? Would we meet new friends in Africa? Would we even have a school in Africa?

It was 1961, and we lived in a very small town in the Deep South. I had not been exposed to a lot of black people except those who helped us on the farms and in our houses. Although segregation was still very strong in our little town of Stone Mountain, I had been somehow protected from the ugly aspects of racism. There was an attitude of white superiority that I recognized in my parents and other white grown-ups, but I did not learn the real hatred of racism and prejudice that some others had developed during that time.

I was also worried about living with the "natives," as my parents called them in the early days. Would they be kind to us? My only concept of Africa was from the Tarzan movies I had seen a few times on someone else's television.

For the most part, Mother thought watching television was sinful because of all the bad things you could see. I saw some pretty bad things on Tarzan. That's when I started worrying about whether or not I would be eaten by lions, and whether or not the natives would be friendly. When I asked her those questions, I received what was to become her usual reply to my questions of concern: "We're in God's hands now. He will take care of us." That really didn't ease my mind, but I knew when to keep quiet. Maria and I, sitting in our little upstairs bedroom with Mother and my Dad that hot summer night, were eager to get some more of our questions answered. Maria started in first asking Mother and Dad questions about the school she would be attending.

As Maria started talking, Mother interrupted her. Looking directly at Maria, and in words that seemed blunt and cold to me, she told Maria that they had just found out that she would not be able to go to Africa with us because there were no mission high schools where we were going. Maria's face went blank. I looked from Mother to Maria, then to my Dad. Surely he would say something to correct this awful situation, but he just looked away. He had tears in his eyes.

I knew a term on the mission field was four years with one year of furlough. Furlough was when we got to come back home for a year. That's when we would next see Maria, I thought to myself. Four years in between was a long time—for me and for her. Suddenly, I felt a surge of anger and sadness that I had not experienced in quite some time. It swelled up inside me until I thought my chest would explode. The thought of losing my hero, my protector, and my confidante terrified me. My big sister was my secret shield between me and Mother.

There were a lot of tears that night after Mother and my Dad spoke to us. Maria cried. My Dad cried. I can't remember if I cried, but my anger, fear, and sadness were intense and I "went away."

"Why can't she go? It's not fair and I don't want to go if she can't go." It was a child's logic; I do know that the one thing a child will hold on to and fight for is his or her family, the one thing they can call their own. It is "supposedly" their God-given right. And I wasn't going to let anyone break my family apart. Also, my sister, Maria, was the strong, determined one. I thought she would be devastated, and I expected a real set-to before it was all over with. But it never came from my sister.

Maria was the tomboy in the family. She lived for adventure. Mother could never get her in a dress without threat of punishment. I expected more of an argument from her on this issue. She argued with Mother about which came first after dinner: doing dishes, or thirty minutes of practicing the piano. But when it came to speaking up for herself about being left behind, she became quiet and wouldn't talk about it. She wouldn't even talk with me about it. I did not understand what was going on with her. As a matter of fact, I didn't understand much of anything that was going on with Maria, or Mother, or my Dad those days.

If she didn't go to Africa with us, Maria would be nineteen years old when we saw her next. For a moment, I thought about what it would be like not to have her around. But what really grabbed my heart as I listened to Mother speaking was that I was fiercely afraid of losing Maria. I couldn't imagine my life without Maria. I was told she would be living with a family who went to our church. I didn't know the family, but they had a daughter close to Maria's age so maybe she wouldn't be lonely. Still, I was very troubled about leaving my sister alone.

We had just spent the past three months packing five fifty-gallon metal barrels, one in each room of the house. Those barrels held kitchenware, medicine, clothing, shoes, and anything else we thought we needed to take for each of us to last the next four years. What a challenge it was to guess what we would need to pack for the next four years for three growing children and two adults! How do you buy a pair of shoes for two three-year-olds that will fit them when they are seven? What about buying a coffee pot when you don't know if you will even have electricity? So much was unknown, so my parents pretty much winged it. I had these thoughts of getting over to Africa and running out of food or clothes, or clothes for my dolls. But Mother assured me in her usual manner.

She quoted to me once again, "But my God shall supply all your needs according to his riches in glory by Christ Jesus." Philippians 4:19 KJV. Maybe, but that was the problem with the Bible for a kid of my age and smarts, it just didn't speak my language.

Once the barrels were packed and sealed, they were shipped across the Atlantic Ocean scheduled to arrive at the Port of Lagos, Apapa, Nigeria. The journey usually took around five to six months at sea; however, upon arriving at the harbor, the barrels could be vandalized, stolen, or lost—never to be found. One missionary family received their barrels two years after they arrived on the field. Another family found theirs with such terrible water damage that all contents had to be thrown away. Many items got confiscated "fo de goveenmint" (for the government). That meant whatever security guard was checking our barrels at customs and saw something he wanted for himself, he would just take it. With all the packing going on, as well as finding a home for my sister, the reality that we were truly leaving for Africa became clear to me.

After a rather lengthy and tedious acceptance process, my parents were received into the Sudan Interior Mission. It is one of the largest interdenominational missions working mainly in Africa, but also in several other countries across the world. My parents had completed the "deputation work" for their first term of four years.

Deputation is somewhat like marketing yourselves and what you as missionaries will be doing on the mission field. It is composed somewhat like a very time-consuming and tiring job— unless you have a rich uncle; and, it was usually done before you leave for your first four-year term and during every following furlough. In addition to the monthly prayer letters sent to all of our supporters, friends, and families, during furlough there may be lots of interstate travel to visit your supporters at different churches. That travel most often requires the whole family's attendance. At least, it did with my family.

"These people are paying our expenses for four years and they want to see you," Mother insisted.

So my Dad would speak at whatever church we happened to be visiting that Sunday morning, and we would all line up after the service in front of the pulpit. Then everyone would come down to shake our hands and pray with us. When a person, or a couple as in my parents' case, was accepted by our mission, it was up to the newly accepted missionaries to obtain their own financial support for as long as they were on the mission field. The process of acquiring these funds was another part of deputation work. The new missionaries would also use this time to speak to the people at the churches and explain the work they would be doing for the mission, including where in Africa they would live and what their specific needs would be for the next four years. This financial contract was usually good for one four-year term. It would hopefully be renewed four years later when the missionary was back home on furlough, the missionaries' one-year, so-called rest break, which was hardly a rest.

My Dad had a great sense of humor and was a very compassionate man. He loved to play the piano, go fishing, and he was a master printer by trade. He was one of those people with whom everyone got along. He was genuinely liked by all. Since my Dad and I were so close, he had a nickname for me, Pixie, because of a little point on the top of my right ear. He probably called me his little Pixie more than he called me by my real name. Anyway, I was his Pixie until the day he died.

Mother was the youngest of ten, five girls and five boys. She didn't have the easiest life, as she lost her own mother when she was ten and did not have a good role model after that. Her nine brothers and sisters raised her, some more than others and some with more love and care than others. Her father, my grandfather, was not what I would call a loving man, but he worked hard and cared for his big family as best he could. Mother married at eighteen and had Maria on their first anniversary. My Dad was in the Navy. Five years after Maria was born, I was born, and when I was six years old, my parents produced a healthy set of fraternal twins, Edward and Ann. This happened the same year they were accepted into their first year of Bible college in Chattanooga, Tennessee, in preparation for going to the mission field.

I became aware, at a basic level, of my parents' religious beliefs when I was around six or seven. I remember going to church regularly, every Sunday morning and evening. We also went on Wednesday night and had nightly family prayers. I also remember seeing my parents reading the Bible all the time. It was around their second year in Bible college when they "got the calling" and started preparing to go to the mission field. At this point, they did not know they would be sent to Africa.

My Dad was rather quiet about his beliefs and didn't engage in conversations much about them. On the other hand, Mother was always trying to teach us something, especially if it pertained to how children should behave. Maria and I were taught never to talk back to our parents or any adult, no matter what, or we would be whipped with the belt, spanked, or slapped in the face. We were all taught to eat everything put before us and not leave the table until we did.

One of the many verses that Mother always quoted was Proverbs 13:24 KJV, "He that spareth his rod, hateth his son..." Mother never spared her rod, only her rod was a belt. She believed, along with many other fundamental Christians that we come into this world born in sin and with a sinful nature. This willful spirit that we all have as babies and children must at some point be broken and turned over to God. Mother was a strict disciplinarian. I can remember only one whipping from my Dad in my life. And he ended up not saying a word, but crying right alongside of me.

When Mother was raising me, she had a particular way of expressing her displeasure with me. She would look me directly in the eyes, raise high her left eyebrow, and at the same time lower her right brow down over her right eye. During this odd facial contortion, her forehead would become furrowed and her lips as tight and thin as a stretched rubber band. I used to think that her face had gotten stuck because it stayed like that so much of the time with me. There was no way I could have been that bad that often. Mother looked mean and cold when she made that face, and I knew I was in trouble. Maria and I called this look the "ole evil eye," and we avoided being the recipient of it at all costs.

Mother could give us the "ole evil eye" in a split second, and its message was conveyed equally as fast. Her message: "You are in trouble. Straighten up or you will get the belt." The message I received was: "I am unacceptable. I am unworthy. I will be punished in some way." Those messages gave me the feeling of being unloved. Mother's look was rarely given as a warning. It meant impending doom, and I had no doubt that a whipping or some form of punishment would follow. I usually received these looks when verbal communication was not convenient, like sitting at the dinner table when we had company or squirming in my seat during Sunday morning church service.

One morning, during the pastor's opening prayer, I felt a strange sensation in my body. I opened my eyes and there it was—"the evil eye" upon me. I couldn't figure out what I had done to displease Mother. Mother would tell me I had displeased God. It was difficult to understand what she meant. And it was hard to see her disappointment in me. Over time, I learned to cope by escaping the feelings that these looks would give me, as well as the licks of the belt that would follow. I would "go away" in my mind. By holding my breath, spinning until I couldn't stand, or some other means of hurting myself, I would get all of my attention focused inwardly, in that big black hole where there was nothing. All I felt was numbness over my whole body.

Be Kind

*Everyone you
meet is fighting
a battle you know
nothing about.
Be kind.
Always.*

— Ian MacLaren

arrival Nov. 8, 1961
        June 1965 → USA furlough || 3⅔yr.

            3 yrs. 8 mo. → furlough

2 mo. 1961
    1962
    1963   furlough June 1965 – end July 1966
    1964   1 yr. 1 mo.
6 mo 1965   4 mo
                                                      1 yr
depart June 1968   5 mo
                    = 3 yrs 2 mo.

August 1966 – June 1968 – 1 YR. 8 mo-
"African" + "Nigerian" intertwined as if one + the
        same, without distinction.

Aug 1966   3 yrs. 8 mo
Aug 1967 1   1 year 9 mo
                      _____
Dec. 1967 4 mo
                      5 yrs 5 mo.
June 1968 5 mo.
                         TOTAL

Chapter Two

Arriving on the Dark Continent

The KLM propeller jet arrived safely at the Lagos airport on November 8, 1961. We spent a few extra days at the Mission Headquarters in New York City for last-minute details like getting our passports and tickets. We also had to get a medical check-up from the mission doctor. Every missionary and missionary child was required to have a check-up upon both leaving and arriving back in the United States. That visit typically included shots—shots that made your arm so sore you could hardly move it, and shots that gave you a little bit of the sickness that they were supposed to keep you from getting.

My parents had often called Africa the "dark continent" during our visits to the churches. Doing so had made it sound like such a scary place. I would later learn that the term "dark continent" referred to the mystery of the land itself and the lack of the ability to actually map the continent, rather than the darkness, or impermeability of the African soul like so many believed. The term, dark continent, was made popular by Henry M. Stanley, in his account, *Through the Dark Continent*, in 1878. But walking through the open-air Lagos Airport on a day that the sun shone so brightly it made your eyes tear up and seeing the people dressed in the most colorful clothes, I couldn't find anything dark and scary about Africa.

"I git fo you, Masta!" An eager Nigerian ran up to my Dad and grabbed the suitcase out of his hand as we passed through the airport. Before we were able to catch our first breath of the suffocating hot and humid weather for which Lagos is known, there appeared at least a score of the locals, all ages, trying to carry our bags. I saw a little Nigerian boy my same size walk right up to Mother and take her suitcase from her like it was a feather pillow. I wondered if he was ten as well. I smiled at him, and he giggled. The heavy heat, a cornucopia of the richest of smells, and all of the strange people pushing against us was overwhelming. They were trying to help or assist us in any possible way in order to receive the obligatory dash (what we call a tip). If they did not receive one, they would look at you and say, "Dashy, gif me dash."

I took it all in: the strange noises from the cars, the people speaking in a strange language, the beautiful ebony faces against brilliantly colored robes that billowed in the hot, smelly breeze. This was my first introduction to the culture shock I would experience over the next several years. (It would also include going back to America after four years in Africa.) No one had prepared me for this. I simply did not understand what it all meant, and I certainly did not grasp how it was affecting me. It was if a door had dropped down upon leaving the plane, shutting off everything West behind me, everything in front of me now African, new, strange, and a little frightening. I would live out my childhood and graduate from high school in Africa, but I knew my life had already been changed forever.

My thoughts were interrupted by a shaking yet familiar voice and command which jerked me backed to this new reality.

"Cheryl, hold the twins' hands and stay right behind me. Don't talk to anyone," Mother commanded. I had heard that tone of voice before and knew a sharp backhand across my face would be the result of not paying heed to her commands.

"Why do they call you 'masta,' Dad?" I asked. No response.

After yelling my question to him several times in my high shrill voice, he turned and responded to me quietly. "Sister, not so loud! The African people look up to white people, and it is a sign of respect to call me Master."

Despite being born in the south during the fifties, I was not prepared for the blatant sense of superiority I would witness between the missionaries and the "natives." My parents and other people their age, people born in the early 1900s, were a product of their era to a certain degree, but the racial hierarchy here was so apparent I could see it plainly, even at my young age.

While my parents were trying to maintain custody of our bags, the twins, and me, I noticed a strange looking white man, painfully skinny, fighting his way through the crowd. In a language I had never heard, the stranger spoke harshly to a Nigerian who was in a game of Tug-O-War with my Dad over one of our suitcases. The poor Nigerian, who was only trying to help, looked ashamed and quickly disappeared into the crowd. At the same moment, another Nigerian in a starched white shirt and white baggy shorts appeared. He quickly gathered our luggage and placed it in an old Volkswagen van. We crowded into the van afterward. I soon learned that the skinny white man was named Mike, a missionary from New Zealand, a Kiwi. He was there to take us to the place where we would be staying on the mission compound. He spoke English, but he had a very strange accent, one I had never heard of before. It took several minutes before I could even tell it was English. As I got to know him, I really enjoyed listening to him speak. My Dad told me he had an Aussie accent, but we found out that Aussies came from Australia, and Kiwis were from New Zealand and had their own accent. The Nigerian man in the starched white baggy pants, like those I had seen on Tarzan, was named Joseph. He worked at the mission with Mike. Joseph called Mike "Masta," like the Africans had called my Dad earlier. Mike told me to call him "Uncle Mike." I thought all these new titles quite strange—Master and Uncle. I knew Mike wasn't my uncle, and they didn't tell me his last name so I could call him Mr. I saw Mother shake her head up and down, and I knew that I had better do as he said.

The van ride from the Lagos Airport to the mission compound was out of this world, certainly not the world I had come from. What a wild ride! The windows were open because there was no air conditioning. The temperature was over one hundred degrees, so the hot wind blasted you in the face. I sat by the window with my head hanging out like a dog. But since no one heeded the lane markings, you had to be careful for both on-coming cars and especially passing cars which would come within inches of your own car. We had our share of humidity in Georgia, but nothing like I was experiencing that day in Lagos. My dress was sticking to my skin. I looked over at Mother, and she was putting on her sweater. At first, I couldn't understand why she would be doing that, but then I saw that her blouse was so wet you could see right through it, and I realized she was trying to cover herself. So much for the way she trained Maria and me to be ladies, "Ladies don't sweat, we glisten." We were all downright sweating like pigs in the sun. Besides her, Ann's hair was wet, and it hung limply down around her face. The heat and the long trip combined gave me a feeling of overall exhaustion. Still, my eyes could not take in enough as we drove along. I was in a state of mild shock, exhausted and exhilarated.

Everything I saw was new to me. The roads were very narrow and had no lane markings. And since Nigeria had been a British colony before 1960, the cars drove on the left-hand side of the streets. Looking out the window, I was in fear the whole way that we would have a head on collision with the oncoming cars, that is, when they drove in the correct lane. There were goats running wildly among the cars. Sometimes children would be chasing them. Women would be sitting along the side of the road bathing their babies in little wash basins. Instead of using a washcloth to wash their faces, they would pour water over their heads, and wipe the water away with their hand in a downward movement over the baby's face. The babies squealed with delight while the mothers would talk with the other mothers next to them.

On that ride, I was also introduced to the African beggars. Until that point in my life, I had only known about bums. I had seen a few of those walking the rails across the street from my house. African beggars were the same in that they were the homeless and shunned by most of society. They were different, however, in that many of them were living with the deformities of leprosy, and while not contagious were still considered "unclean" by society. They were not only shunned, but scoffed at, and often spit on. Whenever a *bature* (ba-tour-a), the Hausa word for white man, stopped at a stop sign, the beggars would try to gain access for a *dash*, or a financial gift. Running to the car, they would put their hands into the window, and shout, "Ples, madam, I beg, gif me dash. Gif me penny!" At times, we would have as many as nine or ten hands banging on our windows begging for dash. If you gave to one, you must give to all or it would cause a small riot, so we would have to roll up our windows. This saddened me as I wanted to give dash to them. My Dad told me that I had a soft heart and didn't understand the bigger picture of giving to every beggar we came across.

The Africans, wrapped in brightly colored fabrics, darted in and out among the cars like the balls in a pinball machine, all competing for road surface. I saw a man relieving himself on the corner stone of a new modern building. I laughed out loud, but when Mother asked me what I was laughing at, I didn't say anything. The strange, savory smells of the food cooking over open fires along the side of the road were pungent and tickled my nose. I immediately felt hungry. A woman in full African dress with a basket of live chickens on her head rode by on a bicycle. I was amazed at her ability to balance it all. The happy smiles on the many shiny, black faces were a stark contrast to the abject poverty that was so evident at every turn. These were the faces of a people I would soon come to love and respect.

"Cheryl, don't stare at *those* people," Mother hissed in my ear as she pinched my leg. My gaze was only momentarily diverted from the long, flat, and bare breasts of the women as we passed the Yabba Market. Bodies weren't shown in my family; they were hidden and treated with shame. These women were proud. I was both embarrassed and curious at their lack of modesty, yet thought it would be rather nice to walk around that proud and free.

"Boy, I bet she has to roll those things up like window shades to get her bra on," laughed my Dad. He knew, of course, the women never wore bras, but Mother ruffled and replied in feigned embarrassment, "Oh, Rolan! Don't talk like that!" She always said that, and he was always saying little things to tease her. He really used to get her goat when he would fart in front of the Africans or our family. But the Africans would laugh and laugh.

"Oh, Rolan, don't do that!" Mother would say.

My Dad had a wonderful sense of humor although he could be a little irreverent at times.

Mother and my Dad were straight-laced and reserved when it came to the subject of naked bodies or sex. I don't ever remember my parents walking around even partially clothed. Bathing was always a private affair. We never bathed with my parents unless it was when I was too young to remember. Sex was never talked about. As a result of these things, I learned to be very modest about my body. I remember in fourth grade—all the boys and girls were told about reproduction in a class at school. We were to be shown a movie made by Kotex and had to have our parents' permission. The boys saw the movie: *What Happens to Boys,* and the girls saw: *What Happens to Girls.* Mother would not allow me to see it. She said it was the parents' place to speak on such matters to their children. But for some reason, my parents never got around to that discussion. That day, instead of watching the film, I had to sit in the Library and write a book report on Human Anatomy.

Mother had quite a straight and narrow system of beliefs and some pretty strict rules when it came to codes of dressing and showing ourselves. Maria and I were not allowed to wear shorts. Maria could not wear make-up. We could wear jeans when we rode horses, or "pedal pushers" when pants were required, but for the most part, we wore dresses like proper young southern ladies. This caused arguments between my sister and Mother.

Maria was somewhat of a tomboy and she was always doing tomboy things that required pants. But Mother stood firm as she believed dressing appropriately, among other things, would set us apart. We were to serve as role models, as believers in Christ. We also weren't allowed to attend dances or go to the movies. "Remember Matthew 7:20: 'Wherefore by their fruits, deeds, ye shall know them,'" Mother used to quote us from the Bible. These were just the values and belief systems upon which we were raised. And it was quite compatible with the value system of the mission they had just joined.

~ ~ ~

The stress of the long journey to the mission was getting to all of us, and we had a few more miles to go before arriving at the mission guest house in Yabba. The twins were whining, frightened, and exhausted. In spite of the fact that my parents appeared brave and confident, I wondered if they feared that they had possibly made a wrong decision. I could see worry lines on both of their faces. I stopped gaping at the scenery and began to worry.

I knew my parents' calling was clear to them. They could quote the book, chapter and verse, from the Bible to support their calling. This was what missionary life would be like for them. They believed their cross to bear was giving up their children and dealing with the hardships of living in another culture. They had already left one child in the United States for four years, and the other three would soon be off to boarding school for nine months out of the year. For me, I hadn't a clue as to what the future might hold. I had no choice in the matter. Did anyone ask Maria or me if we wanted to up and leave our home, family and friends? No! All I knew was not to get in the way of their doing the Lord's work. I must follow the rules put forth by my parents and the mission. It was God's will.

My duty was to do as I was told and be a good Christian girl, but I was never really sure what being a good Christian girl meant. It was like the "C's" I used to get in "Shows Self-Control" on my report card during my elementary school years. What the heck did that really mean, and how does any kid get an "A" in self-control? I wasn't a problem child; I simply couldn't sit still for long periods and, well, I did enjoy a good conversation from time to time. Nonetheless, I knew that I was to be strong and not get in the way of my parents' mission duties.

My private worry session was interrupted when the van swerved, and we made a sharp turn. At last, we had arrived at the Yabba Mission Compound. The sign outside the gate said:

YABBA GUEST HOUSE
In the name of Jesus,
Welcome

This was the compound where we were to stay until my parents' home became ready a few miles away in a suburb of Lagos called Mushin. The compound at Yabba was a formidable fortress enclosed by a high wall of cement and stone and included broken bits of glass intentionally inserted to protrude menacingly along the top. The Nigerian guard was called "my guardi," as were all of the Nigerians employed to watch all mission compounds day and night. Were the natives that unfriendly? I wondered why these guards and the obvious "Keep Out" walls were necessary.

As it turned out, there was a lot to do to prepare for moving in our new house, so I was allowed to stay with my parents for the next several weeks. I would start at Kent Academy (KA) on the first of January, which would come soon enough. I would fly six hundred miles north of Lagos, to a small village called Miango in Plateau State, central Nigeria. KA was owned and operated by the mission, and at that time, only the Missionary Kids (MKs) of our mission faith could attend.

The Yabba Guest House was a simple place. It was a guest house for missionaries coming from or going to New York, passing through Lagos, or coming to Lagos for other reasons. In the main living room, or meeting room, there were easy chairs placed in the shape of the letter "U." In one corner there was a small pulpit for Sunday morning services or other meetings. In the other corner, there was an old pump organ, the same one that I'd soon discover was used for Sunday night Sing-Song and any other time that music was required.

Sing-Song was somewhat of a social event for the missionaries, a chance for them to get together each week after the Sunday evening worship service and sing hymns for a half hour to an hour. Sometimes other people, talented if you were lucky, got up to sing solos, duets, or whatever. And, of course, refreshments were served, though never alcoholic.

The easy chairs were built for function as opposed to comfort, typically a covered foam rubber cushion on slats over stretched linear springs. There were two large ceiling fans, supposedly to move the hot and typically humid air, but they didn't have much of an impact on the tropical heat. Although there were a couple of electric lamps, mostly there were oil lamps for lighting at night. Electricity at Yabba relied on a wing and a prayer, far from a promise in those days.

Lots of windows filled the living room, but on one wall in between the windows were shelves and shelves of books. One could find all kinds of books and magazines, especially *National Geographic*. These gave the room a musty smell, especially in the rainy season. The meeting room opened into another room that had a long table for dining. That was where we ate all of our meals, family style, along with the other missionaries on the compound.

Someone was always in the living room reading, so the twins and I had to be quiet as we walked through the room. Mother was constantly telling the twins to be quiet. But aside from that room, there was really not another indoor room for us to relax indoors, and we weren't accustomed to the heat enough to venture outdoors yet. About the only outside entertainment for us was chasing the lizards. Big things, they were about a foot long with bright orange heads, black bodies, and orange tails. They would lie in the sun, appearing to be asleep, but when Edward would approach them, they would take off like lightening. Ann would laugh her infectious laugh and take off after the long-gone reptiles.

My first night in Africa was not a pleasant one. There was only a short time, five weeks to be exact, before I would be leaving for my first term at boarding school. I was still grieving the loss of my older sister, and the fear and dread I felt at the thought of leaving my parents and my little brother and sister were excruciating. I didn't want to go to a new school alone in this strange new land when I had never been away from my parents before in my life unless it was with my grandparents or close family. I wasn't ready for this. I asked my parents if I had to go away to school. Their response was that Kent Academy (KA) was the only option.

It was decided that my younger four-year-old brother and sister would go to a British preschool in Lagos. This would pre-pare them for being away from my parents and would also free up some time for Mother and her mission duties.

"What I really want for Christmas is to go to the British school with Edward and Ann," I told Mother and my Dad on Christmas Eve, my departure date looming heavily on my mind. I had visited their school with my parents and found out kids my age could go there as well.

"But the British school is not a Christian school," they reminded me. Actually it was a Catholic School. "You need to be in a good Christian school."

Being in a Christian school was of utmost importance to the mission and, therefore, to my parents as well. True, the twins were only going to be in the British school until they were old enough to go to KA; but I was lonely and fearful of the unknown. But that was the whole reason Maria, who was left in the States, was not allowed to come with us to Africa. She would have gone to Hillcrest, an interdenominational Christian school. When that wasn't good enough, she was left at home in the states to go to public schools, where religion was not even part of the curriculum.

Hillcrest High Interdenominational School, the school she would have attended in Jos, was an interdenominational Christian institution just twenty miles from KA, where I would be attending elementary school. The school was well established, with fully developed grades from one to twelve. Maria would have been acceptable for attendance in the school had our mission allowed it. But because of a few theological differences between some people in a couple of the missions in other denominations, SIM made the decision to keep our missionaries' children out of the school. Because of these differences, Maria and other kids like my sister were left at home in the states to go to, of all places, to a public school or other Christian boarding schools. The impact of that decision: devastating to Maria, to our family, and I can't speak to how many others.

"What about home schooling?" I had gotten that idea from one of the missionary women who was temporarily schooling her daughter until they left to go back to the States. No, the mission looked down on that, as it took time away from the missionary parents doing God's work. I again begged not to go to KA; but my parents reminded me of my proverbial "cross to bear" and I began to close up. It was clear to me that my parents were not ones that I could talk to. But if not them, then who?

My parents had made this move to Africa sound like an exciting adventure, but now I was losing my entire family and being sent away to school alone. I couldn't talk to my older sister 6,000 miles away, the one to whom I could usually go, and I certainly could not talk to the young twins. The feelings caused my stomach to cramp and my head to hurt. My Dad thought I was sick. Mother thought I was faking being sick. I couldn't trust anyone. Just like that cement wall around the physical house we were staying in, with no windows and sharp glass along the top, I walled off my feelings so that they would not overwhelm me and no one could get to them.

Ordinary Heartbreak

*She climbs easily on to the box that sets her above the swivel
    chair
At adult height, crosses her legs, left ankle over right,
Smooths the plastic apron over her lap while the beautician
Lifts her ponytail and laughs, "This is coarse as a horse's tail!"
And then as if that was all there is to say,
The woman at once whacks off and tosses its
Foot and a half-length into the trash.*

*And the little girl who didn't want her hair cut,
But long ago learned successfully how not to say
What it is she wants,
Who, at even at this minute cannot quite grasp
Her shock and grief,
In getting her hair cut, "For convenience," her mother put it.*

*The long waves gone that had been evidence at night,
When loosened from their clasp,
She might secretly be a princess.*

*Rather than cry out, she grips her own wrist
And looks to her mother in the mirror.
But her mother is too polite, or too reserved, or too indifferent,
To defend the girl.
So the girl herself takes up indifference,
While the pain follows a channel to a hidden place
Almost unknown to her,
Convinced as she is that her own emotions are not the ones
Her life depends on.
She shifts her gaze from her mother's face
Back to the haircut now,
So steadily as if this short-haired child she sees was someone
    else.*

— David Levine

Chapter Three

First Experience with Boarding School

We got up early that morning. It was the day I was to fly to KA (Kent Academy). I had no idea of what a boarding school was like or how it worked. When I asked my parents, they had no clear idea either. So I went in blind.

Mother laid out a new dress and my black patent shoes with princess heels. It was dress-up time. She had also made me a box of brownies to take with me for a snack. After a quick breakfast, I said goodbye to Musa, our house steward, and the twins. I then left for the airport with only my parents. They thought it would be easier on me if

Me, ready to board the plane for school. I was so proud of the Kodak Brownie that Dad gave me to take back to boarding school.

the twins stayed back with one of the missionary families.

The ride to the airport was quiet. Mother tried to make conversation, but my Dad and I were not into it. I was afraid if I said something, I would cry. We finally got to the airport, and the plane was already there.

"I hope we aren't late," Mother said.

"We're just fine, Mama," my Dad said.

And that was about it.

I kept thinking of Maria, wondering if she knew what was happening today. Now I knew how she must have felt when she was removed from her whole family. I missed her like all get out. The pilot put my trunk into the back of the plane while I held on tightly to my brownies. I felt numb as I said my goodbyes to Mother and my Dad.

Leaving my parents for the first time for six months, I climbed from the wing into the little plane, but I was stopped by a call from my Dad, "Wait!" I thought maybe he was coming to hug me one last time, or maybe he had even changed his mind at the last minute about my going to British school. But as I turned, he snapped the camera. My parents always tried to get pictures for their monthly Prayer Letter for their supporters back in the States. This photograph was supposed to show a normal, ordinary missionary phase of life, getting the kids off to school by plane for the next six months. Look a little deeper, and there is the pain of what is really happening: kids being sacrificed for God's work, families being torn apart, tears being stifled to show false courage.

The little single-engine plane, a Comanche 180, bumped as it taxied down the dirt runway. I was alone in the plane with the pilot. As we took off into the hot African sky, he handed me a coffee tin with a plastic top and said matter-of-factly, "If you need to throw up, you can use this." I was mortified. This was only my second airplane flight. The first flight was in the KLM Airlines prop jet from New York, and I hadn't been nauseous a bit. Though this was a four-seater, I didn't have enough experience with flying to understand the difference between the two when it came to inducing nausea. I took several deep breaths of air. "Cheryl, suck it up and get used to it," I said aloud to myself.

This small plane, one of a small fleet the mission owned, was to be my school bus, my transportation to and from school for the next four years. Instead of a typical school bus route every day in America, mine was to be four times a year in a small plane. The plane would pick me up at the station where I would be living in September, take me to KA, then fly me home in December for a couple of weeks of Christmas vacation. In January, I would be taken back to KA for six months. In June, I would fly home for a short summer, and then it would start all over again for the next year. Sometimes the house I flew to in June would be different than the one I had lived in the past September. It just depended on the needs of the mission. This particular flight from Lagos to Jos would be about three hours in the little Comanche, and on this flight, I sure didn't eat any of Mother's brownies. I didn't feel like eating anything.

Sleeping on the loud, bumpy plane would be impossible, or so I thought. I tried to forget about the tears I shed at the airstrip as I was leaving. I tried so hard to be strong and good for Mother and my Dad. I certainly didn't want any of the other missionaries to see me cry. I knew staying strong was part of being a good Christian girl and doing my part to help my parents be good missionaries. In my mind's eye, I saw Maria standing at the train station, not crying as we all left her, and thought how brave she had been. But, I just couldn't keep back the tears. I considered the emptiness I felt now, a heavy weight that covered me like Mama King's heavy homemade quilts on those cold winter nights when Maria and I stayed with her. It finally hit me that I was alone. So I gave in and let myself quietly, yet deeply, cry on the plane until I lost consciousness—the precious peace that a deep sleep, if you wish it, if you really need it, can bring. The next thing I knew, I woke up with the pilot smiling and telling me we were about to land.

At the airstrip in Jos, there was a Volkswagen van and driver to meet me again. The driver introduced himself as Uncle John.

"Welcome to Jos, Cheryl. I am Uncle John, and I am one of the dormitory parents at KA. How was your flight?"

"Fine, thank you." I was trying to be polite. I wasn't at all pleased with this new custom of calling everyone "uncle." My kin were back in Georgia, and these people were strangers, no kin of mine. Nevertheless, Uncle John collected my trunk and suitcase and placed them in the van. Then he and the pilot walked toward the hanger.

"Come on in, Cheryl. You can get a drink and use the facilities before your ride onto KA," the pilot said. I hadn't a clue what "facilities" were, but a drink sounded wonderful. Just then Uncle John walked up and handed me an opened bottle of Fanta. I took a big gulp. It was warm, almost hot. I scrunched my face, and both men laughed.

"You'll get used to it," Uncle John said. "Ice and refrigeration are hard to come by, and besides, it's the British way. They drink their tea hot with milk in it, and their soft drinks warm." Things were certainly different in this part of the world. Whoever heard of drinking tea hot! Down South, our tea was ice cold and sweet!

The van trip to KA was one of the roughest forty-five minute rides I had ever taken, except at the amusement park. It was before the days of seat belts in cars in Africa, and I bounced around so much I felt like being tossed around in Mother's clothes dryer would have been a smoother experience. We traveled over a dirt road filled with pot holes the size of armchairs. There were places where the road had been washed out completely.

We drove well out of the city and passed many small villages along the way. I was fascinated with the gathering of the little mud huts with thatched roofs. People were coming and going from the villages, herding their goats and cows with a stick. The herder never minded the cars coming or going. It was up to any vehicle with wheels to give way to the animals.

Many of the women were bare-breasted and wore only leaves gathered in the front and back of their private parts with a draw string around their waist to hold up the leaves. Others wore the traditional zany, a cloth wrapped around their body and tucked in on itself to keep it up. Some of the men wore cloth wrapped around them somewhat like a loose hanging diaper, and then others wore white shirt-like gowns to their ankles. The dogs that populated the villages were unlike any I had ever seen. They were on the small side, rather skinny, with wiry dark gray hair. They looked more like the wild dogs we would find back in the woods in Georgia, the kind Maria told me never to go near when we were out on our horses or playing in the woods.

As we continued down the road, I could smell food cooking from the fires in the villages. Unusual, inviting smells filled my nose, and it suddenly occurred to me how hungry I was getting after a long day of travel.

Village after village, I watched my new black neighbors with growing interest. I watched the children playing together, hitting rocks with a stick as we would hit a ball with a baseball bat. Women balanced big loads on their heads with babies wrapped on their backs. It seemed such a peaceful life that they lived.

Suddenly, the huts ended, and we turned into the school compound. The sign said simply "Kent Academy." The dirt road was lined on each side with white-washed rocks. I had never seen rocks painted white and used to line the sides of a dirt road. It looked a little strange to me, yet pretty and manicured. I had a moment of panic, however, I kept myself together. There was an athletic field to the right of me and a sign for the Miango Rest Home on my left. The rest home was where most of the Sudan Interior Mission (SIM) missionaries took their annual month vacation. It was also a place for healing and recuperation after an illness or surgery. As we drove into the compound and I stepped out of the car, I was immediately surrounded by white kids from every direction. Kent Academy was a mission school, and as such allowed only the children of missionaries to attend. The little black children had to stay behind the fence. The contrast was not lost on me.

I was the newest kid at KA and being so brought with it much unwanted attention. I was sure they were coming to welcome me, but I was immediately on

This was my first view of Kent Academy when I arrived in the van.

guard. One girl was pulling at my Snow White wristwatch asking if it was "my very own," and another was asking if the dress I had on was a "store-bought" dress. Being shy, I thought these questions were rather rude, and I just wanted to disappear from all of this unwanted attention. All too soon would I be introduced to sharing everything and wearing clothes from the missionary barrels. These barrels were filled by well-meaning church-goers back in the states with used clothes, shoes, and even underwear. I called them Good Will rejects. You'd be surprised what people will send to MKs and missionaries. It wasn't that I was ungrateful. On the contrary, we used to look forward to getting new-to-us clothes in the dorm. But if you asked me, some of it was ready for the rubbish bin.

In Africa, in the early sixties, one of the easiest ways available to purchase clothes was the Sears and Roebuck catalogue and on a missionary salary, having Sears and Roebuck clothes delivered to your home in Africa was a pretty expensive way to shop. I suppose that's why the girl posed the question about my dress when I first got out of the van. The best solution to the clothing situation was that many of the female MKs, including me, learned quite early to become accomplished seamstresses.

Uncle John was taking my things into the girls' dormitory when one of the girls stepped up from out of the crowd and quickly but firmly took my hand. She was short like me, and whispered right into my ear, "Hi, my name is Kathy. It's okay to be shy. I'm shy, too. I know where your room is. I'll take you there."

"Thank you, Kathy," I heard myself say. Her presence comforted me in some strange, small way.

I didn't see Kathy for several days later and then learned that she was two years behind me, in fourth grade, and that she was painfully shy. But for some reason she decided she wanted to welcome me, a stranger, to KA. We became very good friends for the duration of our time at KA.

With a flock of gaggling girls behind us, Kathy led me into the girl's dorm and down an endless hall of white cement walls with wooden doors on both sides. The room assigned to me was on the sixth grade hall. Four girls shared the room. It consisted of two dressers, one of which had two drawers allocated to me, a large wooden wardrobe that I shared with three other girls, and two sets of what looked like metal bunk beds. There was one small mirror over the dressers, and one broom, which we used every morning to sweep our room. We also used the broom to corner a rat should one be so unfortunate as to get caught in one of our long halls. In fact, chasing those rodents would soon become a favorite pastime!

Views of the room I shared with three other girls at Kent Academy while I was in school. There were two sets of metal bunk beds, one wardrobe (which we shared), and a window which separated the two sets of bunk beds. To the right of the wardrobe (picture on the left) is the door going out into the main hall.

"Welcome, welcome, welcome, Miss Cheryl," a high voice sang out. "I'm Auntie Harriett, and I live at the end of your hall. I'll be helping you get settled in and help you with anything else you need. Your other roommates are outside playing, but will be in any minute to wash up for dinner. Oops, there's the siren now." I wish someone would explain this custom of calling everyone Auntie or Uncle. I knew these people were not my kin, they were complete strangers to me. When I asked Kathy about the situation, she softly said, "Because they are *supposed* to be part of our big family." Of course, now I understood. My real family was gone now, and so they were pretending to be my family in their place. No, that was not going to work.

Of course, I wasn't clear where the end of the hall was, or how she could help me get back to my family, but trying to be polite, I replied, "Thank you, Ma'am."

She must have thought calling her "Ma'am" was funny, or that I was being smart because she sort of laughed and then abruptly turned and left the room. And as if right on cue, my three roommates came rushing into the room, the last one out of breath and carrying a tray of clean laundry. They quickly introduced themselves as Mary, Karen, and Becky. Like swarming bees, they combed their hair, were in and out to wash hands, and grabbed what I assumed to be their clean clothes from the tray on one of the bottom bunks. During this dizzying production, they all talked at once to tell me about KA, the aunties, and the "dreaded rules." Thus began my boarding school life of living by bells and sirens, referring to my elders as aunties and uncles, and anxiously wondering what each new day would be like.

I had never been away from my parents alone before that night. I had the most wonderful goose down pillow that a lady from our church in the states had made for me with goose feathers from her own farm. She had given it to me in a *Bon Voyage* shower just before we left for Africa. I actually thought at the time that it was the dumbest gift I ever received. The only reason I had it at KA was because Mother made me take it with me against my wishes. As it turned out that fluffy pillow became a sanctuary for me. I softly cried into it every night. I suffered terribly from homesickness. It affected me mostly at night, on Sunday mornings, or each day at rest hour—pretty much anytime I got still and quiet. This kept up all the way until it was time to go home for summer break in June, six *full* months later.

My roommate, Mary, was the first to notice my nightly crying. She didn't say anything about it to me at first, but I could tell she knew. Her bed was right under mine. She would ask me how I slept and was I having bad dreams. I always told her I was fine. I always thought of Mary as a big sister even though we were the same age. She was very mature for her age, mentally and physically, and seemed like a foot taller. When I hugged her, my head was cradled by her young, yet obvious, breasts. That felt awkward to me but comforting at the same time. I guess I was lucky to have her as a roommate. She was always very concerned about her friends and roommates.

But Mary, Karen, and Becky never seemed to get homesick, and that always made me feel odd, different. Was I a baby to be so homesick? Was something wrong with me? Karen said it was because they had been going to KA since they were in first grade. They knew everybody, and it was like home to them. Karen and Becky were the friendly types, very outgoing and very talkative. They always had friends coming by our room to play with them.

Becky even said she would rather be at KA than at home. I was horrified to hear her say that.

"Becky, you don't mean that!" I said.

"Sure and I do. My big brother and father yell at me all the time to get out of their way. And Mummy's always busy in the village. Here, I have girls to play with all the time. Why wouldn't I want to be here?" she asked. She spoke in a British accent that had been weakened by years away from her homeland.

Her opinion didn't make me feel better. I felt differently from them and didn't want them to see me get homesick. After all, I had only known them a couple of weeks. So I continued to hide my sorrow from everyone.

One of the most difficult aspects of boarding school life was adjusting to the bathroom experience. I was eleven years old, seventy pounds, and shorter than average. Furthermore, I had always been self-conscious about being so small for my age. After Kathy showed me the dorm room, she led me further down the hall to the "big girls' bathroom" for girls in grades six through nine. I was terrified as I looked into a large cement room. The room was painted in two colors. Along one side of the room was a row of exposed toilets, tanks high up on the wall, with chains hanging from them. Never had I seen such contraptions. I had no idea of how to use them. The wall opposite the entrance was lined with four sinks and one long continuous dirty mirror on the wall above them. The third wall held a row of shower heads. That was it. No stalls. No

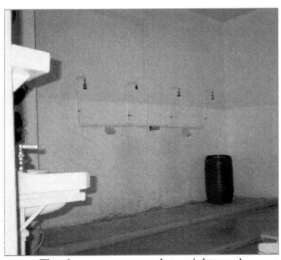

The shower room—and my nightmare!

curtains. The floors were bare gray cement. The room smelled like a mixture of Dettol antiseptic cleaner and dirty clothes. To put it bluntly, everything in the bathroom was done openly. There simply was no privacy. I felt stripped standing there just looking at it, and for the rest of the day, all I could think about was how I was going to avoid the bathroom. It was on that first night after dinner at KA that I was really tested. How could I ever stand naked in a shower room full of girls when, in our home, we just didn't show ourselves at all? This would take some quick thinking. I waited until most of the girls were already in the showers and then got undressed in my room. I put on my robe and waited until I thought most of the girls, including my own roommates, were back in their rooms. Then, and only then, did I walk down the hall to take my shower.

This worked for a few days, but Auntie Harriett, the dorm parent who lived at the end of our hall, soon caught wind of my scheme. Auntie Harriett was about as round as she was tall. She had a kind enough face, with twinkly blue eyes, and white hair that gave her a somewhat grandmotherly appearance. But that's where it ended. You had to make sure you were one hundred percent in line or her anger would flair. I always felt like I was walking on eggshells around her even when I hadn't done any-thing wrong. In fact, that was the way I felt about most all of the KA staff. So Auntie Harriett had a talk with me about what she called my silliness and made me join the other girls in the sister-hood of public bathing.

My first public shower was humiliating. I had never been naked in front of anyone before other than Mother or my sisters. And even that was rare. I walked in the shower room and fumbled with the knot in the tie around my robe.

"Oh, come on in, Cheryl. Don't be so shy," said Becky.

I couldn't take my eyes off the floor mainly because I didn't want anyone to see my tears. I slowly made my way into the showers. Becky was always ribbing and teasing me. I don't think she meant to be mean; but at the same time, I don't think she knew how much it hurt me to be forced to expose my naked self to all of these girls. Tomorrow I would have to face them at breakfast and school, then lunch, and afternoon on the playground, and dinner—before it started all over again. I tried to face the faucet and stand as close to the wall as possible.

Why was I being forced to do this? I felt completely out of control, disgraced, and so different from the other girls surrounding me. They were talking and moving, getting in and out, but I stood still, in one place, frozen. *I don't fit in here. Why can't I be normal like the other girls? Another night of crying.*

I squeezed the bar of soap in my hand. We each had to supply and use our own soap. Mother had provided me with a generous supply of English Lavender by Yardley of London. The smell was comforting to me. It was from home, all mine, and I quickly began washing off the hot dust and memories of the day. I would use English Lavender that night and faithfully throughout all my years in Africa and beyond. As for that first public shower, it lasted about three minutes. And then I was out of there and back in my room, clad from head to foot, and under all of my covers.

Sleep did not come easily for me during my first semester at KA. I cried most nights. There were strange noises, girls coughing, snoring, talking in their sleep, and even girls walking in the halls. I was afraid to walk down that long hall to go to the bathroom that first night, so I just squeezed hard until the sun came up. The night seemed to last forever. I thought about my sister Maria a lot and wondered where she was. I hoped the family that had taken her in loved her and was treating her right. I wanted to know if she missed me. I wondered if she would have liked Africa. Would she rather have come out to Africa with us, her family, or stayed where she was? I was sad that she would never get the chance to see this wonderful country, its beautiful people, and their culture. All these questions kept me awake and there were no answers to them.

The first morning about six a.m., I was surprised to hear one of the aunties singing in a high, shrill voice, "Good Morning. Good Morning. Good Morning." She finished up in a loud, not-so-pleasant voice. "Time to wake up, girls. It's time for devotions." The next thing I knew, she had clicked on the light which was a bare bulb suspended from the ceiling and was placing a Bible at the top corner of my bed right in front of my face. My roommates and I were immediately to start reading our Bibles for fifteen minutes. No getting up first to empty out full bladders or to get a drink. NO! Devotions first thing in the morning!!

I soon discovered that if you fell back asleep, there would be punishment, accompanied by a stern talking to or a guilt-inducing talk from the auntie who caught you. Engendering guilt, whether consciously or not, was one of the house parent's strongest weapons for maintaining discipline among the kids in a mission boarding school, as it is in any religious institution for that matter. How can a child fight his or her perceived concept of the wrath of God? Of course, on that first morning, I promptly fell back asleep not having slept well the night before. Auntie Harriett returned and found me in that sinful state. She woke me up, telling me that she understood I was new, but this was time for devotions, and I had to learn the rules. This time she put the Bible in my hands. I didn't tell anyone that I had never done devotions, that I didn't even know what devotions were all about. Again, I felt isolated and different from the other girls. Was it something my parents forgot to tell me about? Were devotions something I *should* have known about? I made it a point to watch my room-mate, Karen, on the top bunk across from me, and Becky, under-neath her.

I woke up eagerly the next morning at Auntie Harriett's first croaky notes, "Ooohhhh, Good Morning. Good Morning. Good Morning. Time for devotions!" she sang. She would make up songs for everything. Oh my, her voice reminded me of when Mama King, my grandma on my Dad's side, killed the chickens by jerking their necks to break them. They would flop around on the ground for a minute or so making these weird sounds. Boy hidey! I sure didn't like those dying sounds.

Anyway, I grabbed my Bible before Auntie Harriett even got to my room. I started reading a book I couldn't even pro-nounce. It was someone begat this, and that someone begat that… I was struggling. I tried another book in the Bible, flipping pages to find something familiar. I had read the Bible in Sunday School and church, but not on my own. When our teacher had given us verses to look up in Sunday School, we used to see who could make the most noise flipping through the pages to find the verses. That's because nobody knew the order of the books in the Bible to help them find their place. Apparently, in this situation, making noise by flipping pages wasn't funny.

"Shush!" Mary said from the bed below me.

"I am trying to find Psalms," I said indignantly.

"Stand the Bible up on its spine, and let it fall open," she said. I did, and it miraculously fell open to the book of Psalms. Wow, I marveled. How did she know that? I found Psalms 23, The Psalm of David, and read it. I was right proud of myself, and I started reading, even though I had memorized it two years before for a Christmas play. At least, I now knew what devotions were.

And so devotions became another step in the boarding school experience for me, an endless progression of bells, sirens, rules, strange food served on a rigid schedule, showers in public bathrooms, punishments, schoolwork, and a sensation that stayed with me the whole time I was there—loneliness. I learned quickly how to survive. Kids are adept in that way. You learn the system and then try to work within the system the best you can.

One of the most common forms of punishment for both the boys and girls at KA was "sifting sand." During the years when KA was growing in numbers, which basically covered the time span

The sand pit where I spent many an hour.

I was at KA, 1961-1965, construction was on-going. The buildings were made from cement and sand that the local Nigerians made into building blocks. The older boys, seventh through ninth graders, would take the truck to the sand bar a few miles from the school to get a load of sand. When they brought it back, it had to be sifted before being made into cement blocks. This sifting of sand turned out to be the punishment of choice by the powers-that-be at the mission. Say a child at the dinner table reached for the salt shaker and knocked over her glass of milk three or more times a month. That child would be relegated to the sand pit to sift one or more head pans of sand depending on her age, size, or severity of wrong-doing. Say a kid was late so many times a month to meals or to classes, or someone didn't read their devotions in the morning, or worse yet, slept through them, or a kid had too many lost or odd socks in the wash—all of that would relegate a child to the sand pile, sifting the number of head pans to fit the crime.

A head pan was a round bowl-like container that the Africans used in construction work and after being filled, they were carried on their heads by the women. Even with extremely heavy loads, the women could carry these loads over difficult terrain and over great distances. I often watched them with much admiration for their graceful bodies and elegant balance. I prayed I wouldn't land myself in the sand pit, but it wasn't too long before I found myself out there, sifting like all get out.

It could have just been me, but I had the feeling that most of the teachers in the school had a different feeling about sifting sand. I can't recall any of my teachers relegating me to the sand pile for duty. They had their own ways of punishing us, but the sand pile was not among one of their favorite methods. Another thing I appreciated about the teachers was that they were called by their real names. Mr. Jackson was my Science teacher. Miss De Lai was my English teacher. I was okay with that. But all of the other adults were Auntie and Uncle. Auntie Janet was one of the dorm mothers for the girls, and Uncle John worked in the boys' dormitory. Since the idea of calling the other staff Auntie and Uncle bothered me, I resisted. Caught calling them by their first names got me in trouble every time, and I ended up in the sand pit. My sentence: usually one head pan of sifted sand.

The sand sifter was a rectangular wooden frame about twelve inches wide by twenty to twenty-two inches long, and maybe four or five inches deep. What looked like window screen was attached to the bottom. If you were older or had been really bad, you had to sift a whole wheelbarrow full of sand, about three to five head pans. The weather also played a factor in this matter. If it was during the rainy season, the sand was heavy and wet. On those days, it was difficult for us to even shovel it into the sifter. Those clumps of heavy, wet sand just did not want to go through the screen. But during the dry season, sometimes we would get the finest, purest sand, and it would flow through the sifter faster than a streak of lightening. It didn't take long for word of that to spread among the group of "regular sifters." You've never seen so many potentially bad kids sifting in advance while the sifting was good. At one time, I had five head pans sifted for the next time I needed them, another way of working the system.

The whole process of sifting sand was based on the honor system. When we first started sifting sand as little ones, we were monitored by the aunties and uncles to make sure we were doing it correctly, but before long, we basically knew what to do and were trusted to do so. If we were assigned to sift four head pans, that's what we did. And for the most part that's what they got. We were too afraid of the wrath of God or another kid telling on us not to do what we were told.

It was manual child labor, sure as the sun rose; although, I never felt it really hurt me physically. I thought it shaming more than anything else. But I never felt it taught any of us, or at least me, anything. The punishment was not related to the wrongdoing.

As my experience grew, sifting sand gave me quiet time for my own thoughts and time to be away from the noisy crowds of boarding school. The talk, talk, talk of other children sometimes caused me anguish. Sifting was a burdensome, yet pleasant, almost a hypnotic feeling for me when I could be alone.

By the time I left KA at age fourteen, I believe I must have sifted enough sand to build a whole wing on the girls' dorm. It made me feel proud, actually, that I had accomplished something. I did not approve of sifting sand as a punishment because I knew there was an element to it that wasn't right. It was the way it was doled out. It caused us children to doubt ourselves and feel like we were "bad." If I am punished for things I have no control over, or if I am punished for accidents that happen to me, I am not a "bad" child. For example, if I get back one sock from the laundry when I sent in two, the loss was not under my control. It possibly got lost in the laundry. Yet that was one of the egregious infractions for which we were punished. Another one, spilling your drink at the table in the cafeteria more than three times a month. But because we begin to feel like we were bad children, we eventually lived up to that label. Children respond to how they are treated, and that is what I, and many of my other institutionalized friends, began to do.

Most of the MKs I went to school with were born and raised in Africa, or had started KA in first grade. So by the time they had reached sixth grade, they were fully acculturated to Africa and boarding school. Many of them spoke Hausa or the language of their home village. KA was truly their home, as they had spent more time at boarding school than they had at their home with their own parents. In comparison, I came to KA while in sixth grade, separated from my parents for the first time. I wondered if my schoolmates suffered the same sense of abandonment, loss of dignity, loneliness, and confusion when they arrived at a younger age as I did arriving at age eleven. All of us were alone, many without siblings, and without the choice of going back home, but I felt that those of us who came later had a harder time adapting. Attempts to communicate to our parents through our weekly letters about our loneliness or unhappiness with KA or something that was worrying us were blocked completely or highly discouraged from reaching our parents, depending on our ages. On one occasion, I was told by one of the aunties that I should be grateful to KA because a decade or so ago, I would have been left in the states for four years of elementary school like my sister was left during her high school years. I was so furious when that auntie brought my sister into the discussion that tears seemed to come from nowhere and I blurted out, "At least I would have had someone with me." She didn't like that and made me go to my room for the rest of the day. I was angry, so angry, but I wasn't going to let her see it. So I hid myself in my favorite spot, under the covers with my arms and legs around that special goose down pillow. That pillow had become my surrogate sister, and we had a good long talk that day. Talks like those got me through many afternoons at KA.

On this day, I thought about arriving home from school back in Stone Mountain. Mother would have some milk and a piece of fruit for me. She would question me about my day and get me started on my homework. Until I got to boarding school, I never thought I would miss those times. At boarding school, there was no one to talk to about my day. The aunties were too busy and the other kids had had the same kind of day, so I began to notice myself having a conversation with my "selves" (friends in my head that would help me out now and then when I needed help or when I was lonely). It was another step in my journey to isolate myself from others so I would not feel the hurt.

We, as little children, could not understand "God's calling." The calling, the belief in God's will was a theological choice for the missionaries, but to the children of the missionaries, it was quite another matter. The grand calling for some of the missionaries was found in verses of the Bible in the book of Mark, precisely Mark 16:15-16.

> [15]And he said unto them, Go ye into all the world, and preach the gospel to every creature. [16]He that believeth and is baptized shall be saved, but he that believeth not shall be damned.

That was one of the driving purposes of my parents and other missionaries of the faith. There were other specific "messages" from God that clarified the message willing some missionaries to go to the field. So to the parents, the calling to uproot the family and leave was clear. It had to be clear or, hopefully, they would never have left.

To us, the children, who had heard these verses so many times, there was no such interpretation or understanding. There was no explanation of what was to happen in our lives. Being sent away to a boarding school to be raised by strangers and sometimes abusive house parents, to experience culture shock, be stricken by new tropical illnesses and diseases—all that happened to these children would affect them for the rest of their lives. In terms of our parents breaking up their family for the greater good, we had no choice. As a result, I felt I had no control over my own life. Things happened to me that I did not understand. I did things even when I did not want to do them. I did not have the support systems around me that I was used to. Everything was different. Nevertheless, life got easier at KA over time. I did learn the many rules. This was my strange new life, in a strange new country. I went through the daily activities, the movements of life, but I was beginning to lose myself to the loneliness that consumed me. Day after day, I would get up, dress, and be made to eat a porridge that made me nauseous. I would take a vitamin and antimalarial that would usually have me puking by nine o'clock, which was right when school was starting. Then, I would go to school for the morning, eat lunch, and have rest hour. Without air conditioning, it was just too hot to do much of anything during midday. Classes picked back up for the afternoon session and lasted until three o'clock. After three o'clock, the afternoons were free. That free time was filled with job duties of all kinds. If you'd gotten in trouble, there was sifting. We might have piano lessons or piano practice, or any other instrument KA offered. "The Lord had blessed abundantly," and we had almost every instrument in the orchestra, beat up as they were. If it was laundry day, it meant picking up your laundry and putting it away. We also had to take time to learn our Bible verses for the week. Each week we were assigned so many verses or a chapter from the Bible that we had to memorize and on Saturday repeat it to the auntie. Candy Day was something I really looked forward to. Three days a week, each kid lined up at the Candy Room in the main building. Girls had Mondays and Wednesdays right after school; boys went on Tuesday and Thursdays, and then every semester we would swap days. Saturday was Candy Day for everyone, so girls and boys were together. That was fun. The room was filled with shelves of candy tins. It was our parents' responsibility to keep the tins filled. And, of course, Mother kept me stocked with brownies because they were my favorite.

Evenings began at five-thirty when the first siren rang signaling it was time to get ready for dinner, devotions, and study hall. The dreaded shower-time came next and, try as I may, I could not overcome my extreme modesty. It was something too strongly ingrained in me since early childhood. At the end of the day, I would take solace in crying myself into a very deep sleep. The next day, it all started over again.

The monotony was maddening, and my days were empty. In the crowd of kids, I became invisible. I was one among so many. I ceased to exist. This was the part of me my friends never knew. They only saw the friendly, clown side. I learned that to the degree

I could swim nicely along with all the little fish and not make any waves was the degree to which I could stay invisible.

I had been at KA for about two months when one day those feelings became so intense that I felt I could no longer tolerate the emptiness. I had to go somewhere and find myself, to feel myself, to hold myself. I walked away from the noise, the kids, and the buildings. We weren't allowed to go off the compound, but I found myself at the end of the walk on the tennis courts, alone, and protected by a very tall wall that prevented anyone from seeing me. In a maze of confusion, anger and aloneness, without volition, I spun my whole body around and around, arms outstretched.

The tennis courts, my own private place of escape. When I took this picture, I was standing about fifteen feet above the tennis courts as the courts are dug out and are much lower than ground level. When I stood in the corner of the courts (see arrow), I was not seen unless I moved out toward the center of the court.

The hot African sun baked the tar on the courts and its heat rose up under my dress, warming me as I turned faster and faster. I was dizzy, but I kept my balance. My mind was going to places unknown to me. It felt good. Round and round I went, faster and faster, my breath getting hotter and tighter, my mind going to a blank space—no aloneness to hurt me, no aunties, no uncles, no strange kids—just numbness and spinning until I collapsed on the hot surface of the court. I must have fallen asleep, or maybe passed out, because when I woke up I was overheated and my skin was burning. But the experience had given me a strange kind of relief to my suffering, and the feeling I got from escaping was beginning to be addictive. I found myself coming back to the tennis courts every time I had that feeling of non-existence, loneliness, or unworthiness.

~ ~ ~

Sunday afternoons were the best time of the week. We usually had a good lunch, then rest hour from one o'clock to around three o'clock. Immediately after rest hour, we met at the

center of the compound by the big tree or the playground to go on our Sunday walk. This was my chance to get out into the bush to see the land and my African neighbors. We took hikes everywhere. Rock formations formed shapes of animals, such as camel rock because it looked like a, well, camel. Swinging Bridge, from the old tin mining days of the 1930s when the British were in control of Nigeria, hung across a deep gorge with a small

The wonderful Sunday afternoon walks.

river below. The bridge was an exciting place because I had heard stories that someone had jumped off to commit suicide and others had fallen off. When we were lucky enough to go to the volcanoes, we would find interesting igneous rock. The volcanoes were two large mounds side by side that used to be one large mountain before it blew. It was also too far away from the school to walk, so we got to go in the truck—always an adventure. Mt. Sanderson, another mountain we frequently climbed, was a rather small mountain, easily walked, and it was right behind the boys' dorm. From the top, we could see our whole school compound as well as a panoramic view of the surrounding countryside. Sometimes we would ride in the truck to the sand bar where we got our sand for sifting and play in the water. I felt so free on those walks and Sunday afternoon adventures. I often thought of taking off on my own adventure and just living in the bush with the Africans, never going back to KA.

I loved meeting up with some of the Nigerians along the way. As usual, the women balanced their purchases or household necessities on their heads as gracefully as ever. I'd seen them loaded down and with a baby on their backs, they would pick up small items they'd dropped by pinching them with their toes and bringing the item up to their hand without bending over. Over time, I practiced those moves myself and found them very helpful. My friends and I would carry our books to school on our heads because of its practicality and just for the fun of it.

Miango, the village where our school was and still is located, is inhabited by people of the largest ethnic group in West Africa, called the Hausa. Hausa is also the name of the language that is spoken across most of Northern Nigeria. Approximately thirty-five million people speak Hausa in Nigeria, and over forty-one million if you count those who speak it as a second language there and across other West African countries.

I learned just enough of the language to be dangerous, but I loved speaking with them as much as I could. The language is melodic. I especially loved going through their greeting rituals with them. The Hausas seemed to like it, too, as they are a very social group of people. The greeting began as soon as two or more people approached each other, no matter how far away from each other they were, as long as they were within hearing distance. It began with a general welcome.

"Sannu da zuwa." (Hello) The men usually bowed from the waist and the women did some form of a curtsey, more of a sim-

ple bending of the knees as they usually had loads on their heads and/or babies on their backs.

"Yauwa, Sannu." (Hello to you also.)

"Kina lahiya?" (How are you?)

"Lafiya lau! Na gode." (Fine! I thank you.) By this point they may be passing each other on the path or road, but the greeting continues.

"To (pronounced toe), Sannu, Sannu." (Okay, hello again.)

"Yauwa, Sannu." This may continue as they pass each other and until they are out of hearing distance. It is also customary to stop and ask about the family, work, and anything else of interest, which can make the greeting quite long at times.

It gave me a great sense of pride to be able to greet the Nigerians as we would pass them on the paths on our Sunday walks. The little children of the villages lightened my heart in a special way. White people were a thing of interest and intrigue to them. They were fascinated by our clothes and especially our long straight and light hair. I loved how they would run towards us, wanting to get near, only to retreat in haste with fear, possibly of harm, or the unknown. Sometimes, the older kids would make a game out of it. They would rush up to us, and some of our boys would stamp their feet at them. The village children would laugh heartily, immediately turn and run away, only to come back and want the process repeated. I thought it great fun. But, sadly, we were not encouraged to interact with the local people very much. I was not sure why this was the case, but it was a great disappointment to me. Nevertheless, I used to live for Sunday afternoons and those wonderful walks. Looking forward to those weekly walks broke the time up. Before I knew it, April had arrived, and April was the time to celebrate Trunk Day.

The other kids told me that next to Christmas and Going Home Day, Trunk Day was the most exciting day of the year. On a predetermined day during the month of April, it was time to get everyone's trunk or suitcase down from storage in the attic. The trunk was then placed at the end of our bunk beds, and the packing process to go home was begun. The aunties and uncles started the packing process in April because it took anywhere from six to eight weeks to gather all of the person's belongings.

Some may have been loaned out and/or lost in the laundry, and it took time to pack all those belongings for around two hundred kids. Quite a chore, I can tell you. It used to amaze me how many things would end up in my wardrobe that had other kids' names on them, and my clothes in other peoples' rooms.

I wanted to put everything into the trunk right away, as I was ready to go home immediately. However, since it was now April and school was not out until June, only the aunties were allowed to place anything into your trunk. Oh, the temptation of the trunk! The site of it at the end of my bunk made it very hard to focus on school, learn my weekly Bible verses, and even go on my weekly Sunday afternoon walks. But I tried. I wanted so much to be happy, so I could tell my parents that KA was a nice place and that I liked it. I didn't want to cause them concern or interfere with God's work. Time crawled by, but eventually we were all packed and left with a bare minimum of clothing to last us two more weeks, or just enough to fit into our suitcases. I was never the most patient child, so the wait from Trunk Day to the end of school seemed like an eternity.

As a part of the "Going Home Procedures," we were each told of our flight arrangements. Most of the kids knew the routine. I had to be filled in because I was new. The flights going home usually started the day after school let out. It took about five days to get everyone flown to their respective villages, towns, or cities across Nigeria. Some parents lived close enough to collect and drive their children to their homes.

The SIM had a fleet of several single-engine planes, including Piper Comanches, and a Cessna 170, as well as a new twin-engine plane, the Piper Aztec. Sometimes, we knew the name of the pilot and the plane in which we were going to fly in advance, and that just added to the excitement. If not, we eagerly waited to find out with which pilot and plane we would ride home, as some planes and pilots were favored over others. If you were one of the last to go home, which happened to each of us at one time or another, the staff would do special favors for you, like giving you special treats, or throwing a party for your class in their private homes. Sometimes we would go to a teacher's house for popcorn. Popcorn was extremely hard to get in Nigeria in the sixties, so it was a real treat. The smell would spread across the entire compound, and all of our thoughts immediately went to our homeland—America, Australia, or wherever.

Finally, it was my day to go to my new house in Lagos, a coastal city in the southern-most part of Nigeria. I had just completed the first six months of my boarding school experience, and in the process, completed six grade. The location of my house was actually in a suburb of Lagos called Mushin. Mushin was mainly a large, overpopulated residential area with poor sanitation and low-quality housing. Our house was on the mission compound along with about eighteen to twenty other missionary houses, staff houses, and the printing complex. I had not seen the house I would be living in as my parents had moved in after I left for school.

It was a forty-five-minute ride in the van from KA to the airstrip in Jos, and my mind was racing. I had made the trip once before in January, on my way up to KA, and this time I was feeling like a veteran. I had not seen my parents or the twins in six months, and I was excited to see them. I was also feeling nervous and confused. What was this hesitation? Why was I feeling this way? I still harbored feelings of anger at my parents for sending me away and leaving my sister behind in the States, but I tried hard to keep these feelings down inside. So instead I focused on getting through the flight. The flight was rough, and the anxiety of going home was intense. That all changed when I saw my family standing on the runway in Lagos.

Chapter Four

The Niger Challenge Press

After flying over the bush for several hours, our approach to Lagos was marked by indications of city life. Until the previous year, 1960, Lagos had been a British colony and the signs of British control and influence were everywhere: British architecture, British goods in the stores, British cars on the roads, and British accents heard everywhere. Because they had been educated by British teachers, some of the young Africans had British accents when they spoke English as well.

Lagos was the capitol city of Nigeria and would be for several years to come. The city was struggling towards modernism, yet poverty was rampant. Lagos had yet to experience the population explosion that would bring it

My Dad's first assignment when we arrived in Lagos, Nigeria. Left to right: Eric, fellow missionary from Scotland and worked with my Dad in the print shop; Nigerian work assistant; Nolon King, my Dad.

from 763,000 people to over 21 million over the course of the next half century. From the air, I looked down on mile after mile of aluminum, wood, and cardboard lean-tos. I spotted bill-board signs for Bata shoes and Star Beer, with Africans living the high life. British and German cars crowded the streets below disregarding the use of lanes. It was all so exciting to me. I found my stomach tickling from the desire to be down there in the thick of it. At the pilot's warning, I prepared for landing, and then returned to looking out the window. There they were, my little brother and sister, Mother, and my Dad waiting beside the airstrip, waving. I suddenly caught my breath. Was I ready for this?

As I tried to collect my belongings in the plane, I felt all thumbs. On the way up to KA, I was the only one on the plane coming home. On the return flight home, there were a few other MKs that lived on the compound with me. We would soon become good friends. But now I felt only awkwardness as the plane landed.

"Are you feeling OK?" the pilot asked. "Make sure you have everything you brought with you. I'll pull over to the hanger, and your family will meet us there."

I mumbled "OK" and unlatched my seatbelt. My parents hurried over to meet me, the twins right behind them. A little bubble of anger, origin unknown, popped up, but I quickly pushed it backed down. My anger at them for breaking up our family and leaving Maria in the states was still strong. But I was also aware of some embarrassment, and a little joy, as I jumped out of the plane. Mother was first to approach me. I hugged her stiffly, feeling uncomfortable. Then I grabbed the twins, ruffled their hair, and hugged them warmly. I hadn't realized how much I had missed those little guys.

My parents were tan. They'd spent a lot of time out of doors. Even the twins were darker. Ann had a sundress and sandals on. Every bit of skin that was showing was a deep warm light brown. She had gained a little weight and looked so healthy. My Dad stood several feet away, watching me with his kind and loving eyes. When I had hugged everyone else, I ran over to him. He had tears in those big, blue eyes that I inherited as he bent down on his knees and put his arms around me. He sobbed as he held me tight. I had never felt more loved or more confused, and I cried with him. I felt as if he knew my pain, but for whatever reasons, he couldn't do anything about it. In that moment, despite our confusion, anger, hurt, and embarrassment, everything was okay.

"We got a wiener dog! His name is Prince!" one of the twins yelled. That was all it took to break the ice, and I laughed. I have always been an animal lover, and we had left our dog behind when we left the States. This was a peace offering from my parents, and I was grateful beyond words. I couldn't wait to get to our house and meet him.

"I made your favorite meal for dinner—French fries and fried chicken!" Mother said.

"Thanks, Mother," I said warmly. French fries were my favorite food in the entire world and I hadn't had any in six months. I was feeling better already. We spent very little time at the airport. My Dad grabbed the mail, and then we all piled into a little Hillman station wagon that my Dad had bought while I was away at school, and headed for my unknown home.

During the drive to our house, I kept asking my Dad if we could go into some of the towns and villages while I was on holiday. He smiled and said, "Baby, you can go anywhere you want!" Yep, that was my Dad. After about half an hour, I saw a large sign on the side of the road that said, Niger Challenge Press. My Dad pulled off the main road, and we parked in front of a long, two-story building which housed the editorial staff and printing shop. The Niger Challenge Press was where the majority of the printing was done for the mission. Since my Dad was a printer by trade, this building was where his office and print shop was located.

"I will take you on the grand tour in a day or two when you settle in," he said proudly. But he continued the guided tour as we drove further into the compound and rounded the curve.

Coming into view was a smaller building which housed the Challenge Book Store. The store was open to the public. It sold books, workbooks, music, and gifts related to the protestant faith, and to our mission, its values and purpose. It also sold the monthly Christian magazine that was printed at the compound called *The African Challenge*. Its main audience was directed at the educated African, teenage years and up. It was sold at a nominal fee and the magazine ran advertisements to subsidize the cost. It was a successful magazine that attempted to attract young people to Christianity through interesting stories, current events, and even educational accounts such as science features.

We continued our slow drive through the compound. As we passed the bookstore, the compound suddenly opened up into a large oval with houses all around facing inward. There were maybe fifteen houses around the large oval drive, and my Dad drove

Our first house.

around it slowly while describing each of my new neighbors to me. There were a few houses on the outskirts of the center, and that's where our house sat. It occurred to me that our house, the book store, and my Dad's office were all on the same compound. I liked that; it felt secure! We were to be stationed there for the next two years.

That summer, 1962, was exciting for me. My parents and I were both ready to see some of the sights of Africa, and they tried to do as much with me as they could before I had to go back to boarding school. We went to the outdoor markets to buy our foods and meats. The Yabba Market was one of my favorites and one of the most famous for its beautiful fabrics.

We went to the beach on picnics several times. The Nigerians gathered round us and laughed to see us bring food out of our homes, lay it down on blankets, then eat outside on the sandy beaches. They also thought it amusing that we lay in the heat of the day to turn our white skin brown.

Lagos is on the coast of the Gulf of Guinea, the Mid-Atlantic Ocean. In the 1960s, the beaches weren't all that well developed commercially, but there were Europeans and some Americans who frequented them. On one occasion, we had just arrived at the beach. The waves were smooth and low, and I was about waist high in the water when I felt a searing pain across my abdomen. It was a stinging, burning pain on my stomach and chest that wrapped around to my back. I cried out, and when I looked down, I found myself in a swarm of white-yellow blobs with streamers. I'd never seen a jellyfish before, and I didn't know what they were. The pain was intense, like pins and needles sticking me or electric shocks. There were hundreds of jellyfish stretched out across the water as far as I could see. I struggled to get out of the water and back to the beach, screaming for help. Aside from a mild fever and some pretty big red welts that hurt for a few days, I was okay. However, Mother would not hear anything that day but leaving for home immediately. She did not want the twins or me getting back in the water. So we packed up and went back to the compound.

As I recovered from the jellyfish incident, I was looking for things to do around the compound. Not very many children my age lived at the Lagos compound that summer, but there were plenty of things to do. Sometimes I helped out at the day care for the missionaries' little ones. I also played around and went for walks with my brother and sister. Sometimes, I would work in the bookstore for six-pence an hour doing filing or cleaning. That gave me some busy work as well as some extra money for bean cakes or candy. But mostly, I would find a quiet place to watch the Nigerians come and go as they took care of their everyday responsibilities. They were always singing as they worked. Their singing gave me a great sense of peace and happiness. The rhythms of their music, their bodies moving in kind, the bounce in their walk, and the smiles on their faces, were the ways of my new African neighbors. I loved being around them.

My parents had one main houseboy whose name was Musa. He took care of most of the household chores and was somewhat of a supervisor to the other helpers we had at the house. We had a cook, *Baba*, "old man", who came in to prepare all of our meals, as well as a yard boy, James. We also had someone come in and do our washing and ironing. At first, I thought it strange to have so many stewards for one family, but this was common practice in Nigeria. On some level it didn't seem right to me, given the history of the US and slavery, especially in the south where I was from, but every missionary family, single missionary, and expatriate I knew had one or more stewards. It freed them up to focus on their mission endeavors, I suppose. For the locally employed, working for missionaries was considered a good job. It seemed to be a mutually beneficial relationship. And yet, they were paid pennies a day.

As my Dad promised, he did take me out into the villages. About once a week, he would place a book shelf in the back of the Hillman Husky station wagon loaded with all kinds of religious literature including the Bible, little New Testaments, and, of course, *The African Challenge*. He and I would go out into the townships and villages outside of Lagos, open the back hatch, and begin to give out some free tracts, as well as sell some of the other literature. Most of the literature costs under a shilling, or twelve cents. It was great fun because my Dad would let me take care of the money and give change.

Great crowds would gather around us. Most of them would come just to see what the commotion was about and what the batouras (white people) were doing. It was difficult trying to understand their broken English, but I took great delight in talking with them. The Nigerian children in the city were not very shy, unlike the ones in the bush around KA. Here, they would walk right up to me. I had long straight, blond hair, and they would run their fingers through it. Sometimes I touched their hair, too, which by contrast was mostly worn short and curly, if not tightly braided. Their hair sparkled in the sun, and I would bounce my hand gently against it. Then, out of sheer delight and a little embarrassment, we would laugh and giggle. These encounters always endeared me to the African children.

In the natural way of doing things, the young Nigerian males of marrying age, maybe sixteen and over, liked to tease

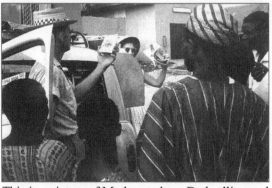

and flirt with the young girls. And one way of flirting (or being fresh) to a young white female was to say, "Ma wife, ma wife." This essentially meant "Be my wife!" or "I want you to be my wife!" When- ever someone yelled it out to me in this

This is a picture of Mother and my Dad selling and giving Christian literature away from the back of their little Hellman car.

way, my Dad would say it was time for me to get in the car as my Dad was very protective of me. I was only twelve at the time, and

58

I thought it was all great fun. But in their culture, girls my age were beginning to be selected for marriage. At the end of the day, we would leave, my Dad and me, taking mental and verbal inventory on an afternoon together of "spreading the gospel through the printed word."

My Dad was always happy after these trips in his little "Hillman-turned-book-mobile," happy to be fulfilling part of his role and obligation as a missionary. I was happy just to have spent some one-on-one time with my Dad. We always gave away more literature than we sold, hoping some benefit would be derived from the process. My Dad always made the comment, "If just one lost soul finds Christ as his personal savior, it will have been worth it." It was difficult for me to understand how these happy people could be lost souls. However, growing up in a fundamental Baptist church, I came to a concluson that it had something to do with repenting of their sins and asking for forgiveness to prevent an eternity of fire and brimstone. I still couldn't relate. Brimstone? I mean, why would a loving God do that?

Our house in Lagos was quite an adventure as well. We had to place the legs of all pantries, appliances, and cabinets in the kitchen in tins of water to keep the ants and other bugs from crawling up to the food. As the weather would often exceed one hundred degrees, the water in the tins had to be replenished daily. This was one of my chores during school breaks. There were always army ants to keep out of the house, though no tins would prevent them from going where they wanted to go. They would make a path from one end of the house to the other and come through in a row of a few inches wide and sometimes up to a few miles long. We learned to live with them. To do otherwise or to try to divert their path would only cause a swarm. And their bite was vicious. I saw on more than a few occasions small animals, swarmed by army ants, die within minutes. It was not unheard of for the little African babies in the bush to be killed by these killer ants as well. After I heard these stories, I had the "night willies" for months.

Lagos was also where I was introduced to African snakes and scorpions. We were always finding snakes in the yard, on the porch, and occasionally in the house, but after my little brother had a run in with a Green Mamba, I became especially cautious of them. Green Mambas can grow upwards of eight feet long, and their venom is highly poisonous. The neurotoxins in the venom can leave an adult dead in thirty minutes, and a child in less.

On the day of the attack, my brother, Edward, around four years old, was playing with his matchbox cars in the shade of the hedges in front of our house. Edward was an active little boy, and when he became too quiet, or Mother had not heard him for a short time, she knew to go looking for him. Mother opened the front door to call him. She immediately saw him under the hedges where a long, green snake was stretched out overhead sunning himself. She screamed for our steward, Musa, to come and kill it. Screaming may not have been the wisest thing to do, but Musa and the steward from next door came running to the front of the house. They both had long sticks and Musa also had his *lunga-lunga* (machete). Musa was never very far from his *lunga-lunga*. Musa told Edward not to move and to keep very quiet. With the ends of the two sticks, the other steward took the dozing snake and lifted the Mamba up very gently at both ends. As he turned around and lowered him to the ground, Musa was waiting with the *lunga-lunga*. No sooner than the head touched the ground, one strong swing, and the head was severed. Edward was safe, and we had our first lesson on how to avoid snake life in Africa. Never play under the lush bushes because, while it is a shady place to play cars if you're a little boy, it offers a great place to sun if you're a snake. The Mamba turned out to be over six feet long and such a beautiful, shimmery green. I thought it a pity that the poor thing had to come to such a bloody demise, but I was thankful for my little brother's safety.

Scorpions were equally as fearful to me as I came into contact more often with them than I did snakes. In Nigeria, we had the large black scorpions that would grow from five to seven inches long. The toxins of these particular scorpions are not fatal to humans, but I have personally witnessed grown men writhing on the ground in pain when stung by one of these devils. Also, there are small brown ones whose venom is even more powerful. My closest encounter with one was, indeed, too close for comfort.

I was getting ready for bed one night and was just about ready to slide my foot into my slipper when I noticed a brownish shape moving in the mid-section. I held it up closer to see what it was, and a scorpion crawled out. I screamed, and Mother, my Dad and the twins came running. Not a lot of excitement happens in the quiet evenings in the bush, but finding a scorpion in your slipper when you are fresh on the field will spark up your evening. I flapped my slipper in the air, and the scorpion fell on the floor. We chased it a bit and were finally successful in killing it. A moment of cheering and dancing ensued as we celebrated another escape from a deadly sting! From then on, I kept my slippers inside of the mosquito net hanging over my bed, instead of on the floor under my bed. But in Africa, everyone gets in the habit of shaking out their shoes before putting them on, just for safe measure.

My house on the Niger Challenge compound that first summer in Nigeria was also my first introduction to people from all around the world. Not only was I meeting many Nigerian friends of the Hausa and Yoruba tribes, but there were missionaries living right in my own compound from New Zealand, Scotland, Canada, England, and Australia, to name a few. As was the custom among the missionary families, the new families were invited to visit the other families for evening meals so that everyone would get to know each other. I learned about different customs and languages at these family meals, listened to different accents, and learned to eat many different kinds of food. It was an education that greatly enhanced what I learned in school, and these visits really began to open my eyes to a world far beyond Stone Mountain, Georgia. These experiences broadened my ways of thinking so that I could see the world as a smaller and friendlier place, an exciting place that I wanted to explore, to visit, and to be a part of it in every way.

Rarely were we invited into the homes of the African staff. But when we were, I especially liked these visits as I got to eat African chop and see the way they lived. Most of the staff lived in homes provided to them outside of the fence at the back of the compound. These houses were nicer than the one they could have normally afforded for themselves. The house itself was made of cement blocks and painted. The Africans didn't usually use doors inside; they used a light curtain that hung between rooms, if anything at all. They typically slept on mats on the floor. The kitchen was small and unlike Western kitchens. There were a couple of cabinets for dishes. Few Nigerians had refrigerators, and instead of stoves they used fires outside. They usually had a hot plate for heating water for tea. You never saw grass growing in the Africans' yards; in fact, each morning the dirt yards were swept clean of any debris. I was told that this enabled the family to easily see any unwanted critters slithering or crawling up to their house. I am grateful to the people of Africa for giving me the opportunity to learn their ways and culture; and I will always appreciate them opening their homes to me and my family.

The Owl Child

In the meadow I see the
   owl-child
resting,
playing,
healing herself
From the dark night.

White-faced wolf
I circle
slowly
closer.
Such joyful noises
she makes and then
remembrances
brings tears

To those wise eyes.
I was not there when
the two-legged ones
cast the stones and
bruised her wings.

But I am here now
and will guard
the night.
And no one will
Ever again hurt her.

The meadow is safe.

—Anonymous

Chapter Five

Second Year at Kent Academy

Oh boy, a full plane. Top left: Me. Top right: Another Kent Academy kid. Bottom left to right: The twins, my sister, Ann and my brother, Edward.

It was the middle of the summer when I found out the twins were going to go back to KA with me. My parents had decided to allow them to go. I was so excited by this news. I had such a great summer at home with my family, and now that it was time to go back to school, I began to dread it. But having the twins with me put a whole different perspective on being at KA. I enjoyed helping them pack and telling them all about school. I tried to keep it all positive and kept a happy slant to it all, making sure they knew if they got lonely or needed anything, I would be there.

We were all subdued as we prepared to leave for the airport. Mother had made the usual brownies for us to take back to school.

When we got to the airport, I think the twins were a little anxious. I knew how they were feeling. I could tell Mother tried to keep the conversation going to keep their minds off leaving. I promised Mother and my Dad I would take good care of them and spend as much time as I could with them so they wouldn't be lonely. The pilot was considerate, knowing I was still relatively new to this whole process, and it was the first time for the twins. He got my trunk and other small luggage packed in as well as Edward's and Ann's belongings, and then it was time to say our goodbyes. I felt a knot in the pit of my stomach. This time, I knew what I was going back to, and I didn't like it. I was too angry to hug my parents, so I busied myself with comforting my brother and sister. They had grown up so much over the summer, and I had grown closer to them. It was going to be a joy to have them with me. They climbed up on the wing of the plane. They looked so small.

This year's flight up to Jos was a lot better, though, than when I flew alone. The twins and I talked, I showed them some sights along the way; we ate some of our brownies, and before you knew it, we were landing in Jos.

After the dusty ride from Jos to Miango, I was told to go help my sister get settled in her dorm room. I wanted to help my brother as well, but since girls were not allowed in the boy's dorm, I could not go into his room. He was just a little kid, and I was in the seventh grade. I could have helped him and comforted him. Sometimes rules just don't make sense when it comes to special situations, situations that need to be handled with a little extra love and care. I watched him walk away with a stranger. He looked back, and it was hard to see him through my tears. Bitterness!

I took Ann to her room, and we got her all settled in. I showed her all around, especially giving her the location of my room, and told her to come there any time she needed anything.

I was glad to have the twins with me at Christmas that year. They were placed into the second grade because of the good education they received at the British school. They immediately cured a lot of my homesickness, as I now had them to focus on, to love, and have them to love me. I immediately took on the role of mothering them. I would meet with them before meals to talk and visit with them. We had to sit by grade in the cafeteria, so I didn't see them much during meals. I would go down to my sister, Ann's room, as often as I could. I would help both of them memorize their weekly Bible verses. I would sit with Edward and help him if he had to sift sand. He and I seemed to keep the sifters pretty busy. I can't remember my sister ever sifting sand, though. I'd do anything just to spend time with them, especially in those early days.

The twins adapted quickly and didn't need me as much as the year went on. Ann, especially, did not seem to go through the severe homesickness that I did or she hid it well. I think the first year at home, and the gradual departure from home to the British School first must have helped a lot. Edward would get bullied sometimes by the older boys or have a bad day in class and come to me after school for consolation. If some of the boys in my class didn't like me or got mad at me, they would take it out on my brother. It used to make me really mad, but there was very little I could do about it.

There was a boy a year ahead of me named Bill. He was a first-class bully. One day, he almost tore the ear off of Edward's teddy bear. Edward slept with his teddy bear and loved it dearly. Edward hid his tears so the boys wouldn't laugh at him and brought the bear to me under wraps the next day to show me what Bill had done. I looked at the bear's ear carefully, put my arm around Edward, and said, "If you let me, I can operate on him, and he will be good as new."

"You can?" His eyes widened through his tears.

"Yep. But he will have to stay with me for a few days. Okay?" My eyes glistened as Edward became the happy, adventuresome little boy I loved so much. I was glad I knew how to sew. These were the times when my anger would rise. I would again feel the rage against my parents for bringing us out to Africa to let someone else raise us, and I would be angry at God for not protecting us like Mother said He promised to do. I still continued my private visits to the tennis courts to console myself, but just as often I had to bottle it up. Nonetheless, having my brother and sister there at school with me was wonderful and often comforting.

The next day, I went up to Bill at school and slugged him as hard as I could. I went for the face, but since he was much taller than me, I only reached his shoulder. I said to him, "You had better leave my brother alone and pick on someone your own size, you big bully." I had fire in my eyes and real anger in my voice, but the hatred I felt in my heart actually scared me.

As for me, I could tell it was going to take a little time to get used to my new roommates. I was still quite shy at that age, and I also had a hard time making close friends. Since I was still new at KA, I didn't know these three girls very well.

Lisa was a nice girl, but she was extremely shy and quiet, also always studying or reading. She often got caught reading in the dorm room when we were supposed to be outside playing or sleeping. We were punished for that if we were caught, which seemed thoroughly unfair. It was hot outside, and the boys were bullies. I knew some of the girls hid in the dirty clothes hamper and read with flashlights because they hated going out on the playground or they were hiding from a mean auntie. Although I didn't mind being out on the playground, I knew some of those girls, and I thought it unfair for them to be punished if they didn't want to be outside. And I sure wasn't going to tell on them. But some girls just lived to tell on other girls. They thought it their Christian duty to be tattletales and report the "sins" of others. By seventh grade, most of us were getting a little too big to hide in the dirty clothes hamper, although I could still fit in quite nicely when I found a real interesting book or just needed to get away from the crowd. And it was also a great place to hide from the wrath of any aunties in chase.

Lisa had been at KA since she was in first grade, so she never showed outward signs of being homesick, but like most MKs, she had learned to hide it well. We all learned to hide our feelings from the aunties and uncles to keep from getting in trouble, and from our friends to keep from getting laughed at. From the aunties and uncles, we were inadvertently taught to hide our true feelings from our parents. Since our letters were censored, we knew what we could and what we could not write home about. And anything what would hurt our parents or get in the way of them doing God's work was off limits in our letters.

We hid our feelings from our parents so they would think we were good little MKs, and at least in our minds, still love us. In so doing, I learned to stifle my true feelings.

Mary, another one of the girls assigned to my room in seventh grade, was the smartest girl in our class. She had made straight "A's" in sixth grade. She never got in trouble. I don't think she had ever sifted sand. She was a good Christian girl and never slept through devotions. She actually read her Bible and prayed every morning. How could I ever live with a person like that without suffering from a terrible case of guilt? Or more to the point, how could she ever live with me? She had the effect of making me feel like I wasn't good enough around her. I could imagine her telling God I was angry at my parents for leaving Maria behind in the states and then maybe God would punish me. I had to learn to keep my anger inside. I felt like I had to look as Christian as Mary. After all, that was my role as a missionary kid: to be a good Christian girl and not get in the way of my parents doing God's work.

Despite my comparison of myself to Mary, some of the most pleasant memories of my seventh grade year would be of the times I spent one-on-one with her. She would offer help when I would have trouble with my school work or when I was upset. She gave her help so willingly and kindly, unlike some of the other girls. Sometimes we might find ourselves alone in our room talking, just the two of us. She had a way of making you feel special when she talked to you. I liked it, but it also made me feel lonely, like I was missing something, like I was missing Maria. Mary was the closest to a big sister I ever had at KA, but I never let her get that close to me.

And then there was Jennifer. She had been at KA since first grade. Being away from her home didn't bother her at all. She could even speak the language of her home village, which I thought was terrific. Jennifer was fun loving and playful, but had her own set of friends. She was always busy with the other girls in her clique.

I felt different from all three of my roommates because they were all young women. They wore bras and stood around the mirror at night curling their hair. I was still around eighty-five pounds, and the only one in my class who didn't wear a bra. Some of the boys teased me mercilessly about that. Furthermore, I still hadn't found my place here. As this weighed heavily on my mind, I returned to the habit I'd picked up the year before of making clandestine visits to the far corner in the back of the tennis courts. It felt good to throw my arms out, and slowly start spinning around and around, faster and faster. With my eyes closed and my face turned towards the sky, I could always count on the African sun to blanket me with comforting warmth. Faster and faster I would spin until I began to see colorful auras in my mind. Sometimes, if I could stay up long enough, I could even make images appear in my mind's eye. And then I would collapse into a heap of hot, mindless, flesh—until I again became conscious of my surroundings and awoke, ready to carry on until the next time. Loneliness was so pervasive in my life that the spinning became frequent. That feeling of numbness was simply addictive.

~ ~ ~

The KA enrollment was around two hundred students when I was in seventh grade and feeding a healthy diet to this many children in Nigeria was no easy task. Even though I sometimes refused to eat the few foods I didn't like, I never went hungry at KA. Two foods I did refuse to eat, though, were the morning African porridge and mangoes. Back home, I was used to grits and peaches. I loved both of them. But grits and porridge and mangoes and peaches were just close enough in taste to set my stomach off. I could not tolerate the porridge and mangoes. Unfortunately, they were required eating, and if you didn't eat what was put before you, your punishment was sifting sand. I tried every way I could to get the porridge down. I put salt and butter on it. I tried milk and lots of sugar, but nothing worked. I tried begging and even outright bribing the waiter with candy or Mother's brownies, or to put just enough in my bowl so I could swish it around and make it look like I had eaten a full bowl. Or sometimes I would swap bowls with another hungry student, taking his or her empty bowl, giving my full one in return.

The mango situation resolved itself. After a few days of trying to force me to eat the mangoes, I threw up the bowl of mangoes along with my whole lunch and started hysterically crying afterwards. I really don't know what came over me. I must have had too much of the strangeness of Africa too soon. Whatever it was, it worked, because from then on, whenever we had mangoes for dessert, the nurse told them to bring me another kind of fruit. The porridge, I got better at trading bowls and dealing with the waiters.

As a rule, we had good food at the school and our dietician, Auntie Linda, was always doing special things for the students, especially around the holidays or significant times of the year. "Hog Days" were an example of special days during the school year. These days occurred whenever the school ran low on meat, generally occurring two to four times a year. Nigerian employees at KA would slaughter the hogs or cows for our meat. The animals were slaughtered in the yard behind the kitchen which was situated next to the upper grade wings of the school. It was a simple process, and they used similar principles like we did back on the farm years ago. The cow or pig was strung up by the heels. Then with a lunga-lunga, their throat was cut to let them bleed out. Their head was then cut off, and a large incision was made down the middle of their abdomen. The organs were taken out, the intestines used for sausage, the liver for a main entrée, and I won't go on, but in Africa, everything was used. I mean everything! And what we didn't use for our food at the school, the workers and their families were waiting in line for what was left over. Nothing went to waste. The skins from the animals were even used. I had a Bible cover and a purse made of cow skin, with the hair still on it.

Since we did not have air conditioning, our classroom windows were always open, and the students usually had no warning when these animal killings would take place. In the middle of a spelling test, or possibly during music appreciation, listening to meditative classical music, we would suddenly hear the blood-curdling scream of a hog whose throat was being hand-sawed by several Nigerian "so-called" butchers. The class would erupt with cries of mock horror, with most of the boys running to the windows for a view of the gory dissection. Meanwhile, the girls sat in their seats feigning disgust, since we'd seen this play out numerous times before. And everyone knew the noise signified there would be bacon and pancakes soon!

It was after Christmas that an event happened which was to change my life. During the year of 1953, when I was three years old, I came down with polio. My back and legs were affected, and I was quite sick for several months. I was a poster child for the March of Dimes, and at the end of the fund-raising campaign I won a walking doll, the kind that wound up with a key and would walk with stiff legs. An ironic gift to give to a child with polio, I later mused. The good news was that I was left with no after-effects except mild scoliosis, and one leg half an inch shorter than the other, causing periodic back aches.

During my seventh grade year, however, I fell on a Sunday afternoon walk, and began having more serious backaches. The KA nurse sent me to our mission hospital in Jos to see a doctor. I was actually relieved when I found out who the doctor would be as my parents were friends with him and his wife. He and his wife had been invited for dinner at our house. So at least he knew who I was. He seemed to be a kindly man and had always reminded me of a rather short Santa Claus without the beard.

It was always exciting when one of the students got to go into Jos, but I was actually a little nervous because I was going to have to stay overnight in the hospital. But as I settled into the dusty van and started talking to the boy next to me, I began to relax.

"Hi, my name is Peter. Why are you going to Jos?" he asked shyly.

"To see the doctor. I hurt my back. Are you going to get your cast off today?" I asked, noticing his ratty looking arm cast.

"Yea, it was a bad break, and they have to x-ray it again. I'm just hoping I can get this cast off," he said. That was about the extent of our conversation, so I turned to gaze out the window and watch with wonder and delight the lives of my African friends. The sun was in its usual brilliant form, my head was halfway out the window, and the wind was blowing my long hair everywhere. KA was miles behind me, and I felt free.

At midmorning, the village women had started making their fires to prepare the midday meal, and the array of smells were tantalizing. The children were running around the village butt naked playing while their mothers worked close by. I loved watching the women pound their grain, potatoes, or yams. They would place their yams or grain in the *turmi*, or mortar, a large wooden bowl that usually sits on the ground, and with the *tab'arya*, or pestle, a long wooden mallet with a rounded end, pound the food to the softness or consistency that they wanted for eating or cooking. And as Africans are known to sing or as I call it, make rhythm, while they worked, soon you could hear songs or simple short melodies that would match the movement of their bodies while they pounded their food. We could hear these sounds as we drove by.

One of my favorite pictures—African women working with the babies on their backs.

It was especially fun to watch a mother using the mallet to pound when she had a baby on her back. This pounding motion would throw her back gently forward and back with each pound of the mallet. The baby would gently and ever so slightly slide forward and back on the mother's back, like the motion of a cradle, putting the baby to sleep. It would always amuse me to see the babies sound asleep in spite of all the commotion going on around them. And I always envied the babies' closeness to their mothers. Many babies stayed on their mothers' backs for most of the day for convenience. This way the mother could do her chores of the day while the baby was safely on her back. There was a major downside to this type of childcare as well.

When a child is very young, the baby's bones are somewhat soft and malleable. When the baby's legs are set around the mother's waist and tied with another wrap cloth tightly, it holds the baby securely, but it also tends to bow the legs when this is done day after day after month after year.

Peter and I arrived at the hospital in about fifty minutes. The van took off and left us on the steps of the hospital. It was only a minute before a nurse came out to usher us into the building. She told me to wait while she took Peter to X-Ray and that she would be back to take me to the room where I would be staying overnight. She came back in a few minutes, took me to my room, handed me a hospital gown, asked me to put it on and left the room. About an hour later, just when I was beginning to think she had forgotten about me, she came rushing back in.

"Hey, Miss Cheryl, I am so sorry to make you wait! My name is Auntie Inez. We had an emergency, and I was gone much longer than I intended. Are you alright? Can I get you anything?"

"No thank you," I said shyly. *What? The auntie and uncle thing even in the hospital? I still didn't like this auntie and uncle thing,* I thought, as Inez explained what they were going to do to me that afternoon. She then brought me a terrific lunch with two desserts.

That afternoon, as promised, they took x-rays and measured the length of my legs, only to confirm what I already knew, that my left leg was one half-inch longer than my right leg, and to see if anything else was wrong other than the curvature of the spine. I stayed in the hospital overnight. I really missed my parents, and I didn't sleep well. The doctor informed me that the next day they would put me in a torso cast from right under my armpits and breasts to just below my hip bones. I didn't like the sound of a torso cast at all, but I was too shy and afraid to ask for more details, so I just kept quiet.

The next morning, I saw the doctor again. I had never been to a doctor without Mother before and I was frightened, friend of the family or not. I guess the doctor noticed.

"Good morning, Cheryl. You look a little worried. Are you all right?" he asked.

I nodded to be polite but didn't say anything.

"Well, I'm just going to put the cast on you like we talked about last night."

About that time the nurse brought in a bucket of water. What is the water for? They hadn't explained that. She then turned around and left the room. I felt very uncomfortable.

"Cheryl, let's take off your gown." He leaned forward, and I backed away. I didn't want to bare myself. I was scared and wanted someone there with me. I hesitated.

"You have to, because I need to put the body stocking on you for the cast." His voice was gruff.

I kept hoping the nurse would come back in. She didn't. He pulled the gown off, but I kept it in my hand to cover myself. His whole demeanor had changed. It felt like he was angry at me, like I had done something wrong. He wasn't smiling and his hands were rough. I didn't understand what was happening. For the entire world, I wanted my Mother with me.

"Step into the stocking," the doctor said. He sat directly in front of me with his legs wide apart.

I stepped in, and the doctor pulled it up all the way up to my arm pits. The stocking covered my whole abdomen and down to the tops of my thighs. Although it was thin, I felt somewhat protected. At least my nakedness was covered. But still, I felt very uncomfortable alone with him in the room. Something didn't feel right. I didn't know what to do. I was still waiting and hoping for the nurse to come in.

"You will have to stand here for quite a while when I put the cast on, to let it dry. And it may get a little warm," he said. As he spoke this, he began to slide his hands over my prepubescent breasts. Instantly, a shock ran through my body and I knew my instincts about this situation were correct. He was touching me in a way he shouldn't be. My body jerked again, but I was in shock. I couldn't move. I couldn't say anything. I wanted to scream, but I stayed where I stood as his hands slid down to my private area. He hadn't even started to put the cast on yet.

"Stop it. Stop it. Just stop!" I screamed over and over in my head. But my body stayed motionless, and I felt helpless to do anything about it. The sound of a freight train ran through my head. The sound was deafening. Why couldn't I stop this? Wait!

Was he really just making sure the stocking was smooth like he said, or was he doing something he shouldn't be doing? As he kept on, I felt all the anger of my entire life erupt. The amount of anger that emerged frightened me. I wanted to kill that doctor. I wanted to kill myself and anyone else in the near vicinity *just to make it stop*. I had never known such feelings. And they frightened me terribly, but he frightened me even more.

"Does that feel good?" his tone was casual. Finally, my head found movement, and it shook violently back and forth. The tears streaming down my face went unnoticed.

"No! No! No!" said my head. It was disembodied. It was not a part of me. Where was that nurse? Where were my parents? I was angry at the nurse for not being there, at my parents for not being there, at the doctor *for* being there, at God for allowing this to happen to me. I was most angry at me for not being able to protect myself from this deceitful, hateful man. *That is when I consciously felt my self-hatred starting to emerge.* And then I remembered the tennis courts, and I held my breath, closed my eyes tight, and froze my body, stiff, hardly breathing, completely still. I felt the old familiar feeling of numbness come over me and I went away. He would not hurt me! I was gone, out of his reach.

By now, the process of "going away" in my mind had become almost routine. It was familiar to me. I didn't do it frequently enough to be noticed, in fact, I hid it very well. But I would do it when things would get overwhelming or I felt out of control. I couldn't have explained it at the time other than to say I let my mind go completely blank. It first started with my spinning round and round until I got dizzy, then I would collapse and let my mind take me to a deep and dark, yet peaceful place. I could see the hole into which I would fall, and I would stay there until I was ready to come out. I could now simply hold my breath and go to that same dark and numbing place, a place where I was not aware of what was going on around me. And I could get to this secret place by just holding my breath and willing myself to be there. My coping ability was getting stronger.

This time, when I came back to awareness, standing there in the hospital room, the nurse was helping the doctor wrap the wet cast around my body. I heard the constant hum of the fan. It was mesmerizing. The cast was hot on my belly, and it had a nause-ating smell. My cheeks were hot and beating, and I had a bad headache. I felt weak in the knees, like I was going to pass out.

"Why is she trembling so?" the nurse asked the doctor as if I weren't there. She had a British accent. I don't remember what he said. To me, he was now a man with no face, no voice, and no hands. I had blocked out the very existence of him, focusing only on the nurse and what she was doing. Finally, the man with no face left, and the nurse finished smoothing out the cast. I had to stand in front of a heater while it dried for a while. I don't remember how long. And then it was over, at least the physical part.

The nurse brought my clothes and helped me get dressed. I couldn't do anything without her help because I still wasn't really present, or fully aware of what was going on. The inside stocking of the cast was still a little wet, and the stocking stuck to my skin. It was rough and bumpy on the outside. When she tried to pull my dress over my head, it wouldn't fit around my waist. The cast was too thick for the size of my dress. When I realized that I wouldn't be able to wear my dress, I began to panic. She already had to cut the elastic on my underpants. She tried to calm me and gave me a hospital gown to wear back to school. She teased me a little to help me relax and said that I would have to get my girlfriends to sign my cast. Sign my cast? I didn't want anyone to see it, much less sign it. It was a reminder of feeling shame, shame that gripped me to my core and would not let go, a reminder of something dirty.

It was very hard to bend over and tie my shoes, and twisting at the waist was out of the question. I felt claustrophobic, and I wanted to scream. I could tell things were going to be very different and uncomfortable for a while, but I had no one to talk to about this. I couldn't write home, wouldn't dare tell the doctor, I was just so ashamed of the whole event I didn't want to talk to anyone about anything related to what happened. I was afraid I may be questioned about it. But why did I feel guilty?

I wanted to tell the nurse what had happened, what this doctor, this "so-called friend" of my family had done to me, but then I thought, she must have known. Surely she knew. There was no way that anyone in the near vicinity didn't know. On the other hand, if she knew, why wouldn't she have come to help? So I was afraid to tell her, and I was too embarrassed. But the embarrassment was nothing compared to the anger and the newfound sense of shame and guilt that had begun clawing at my insides. In spite of that heavy white cast all around me, crushing me, tightening as it dried, squeezing me, I felt transparent. Everyone would know what happened and *they would think that I had caused it.* That's right, I must have done it. I was the bad girl.

Mother always said, "The Lord had a reason for everything that happens to us." What was his reason for this? Had I done something wrong? Was I being punished? Was I just bad? Maybe it was all the sifting, or the times I had slept through devotions. I was taught that Jesus was kind and forgiving, but I was confused. How could He have let this happen to me? What had I done to deserve this?

But most importantly, now I had a secret. Every little girl loves a secret! They will even boast about it in a sing-song voice, "I have a secret, I have a secret, Lala, lala, la!" Why? Because at just the right point, you get to share that secret, usually with someone you care about. It is the buildup of knowing you will be able to tell that someone the secret that brings joy and or release to not only the bearer of the secret but also to the receiver. But a secret never told, is a secret never realized. It grows and festers in darkness and finally consumes the withholder until life is no longer as it was before. Yes. Now, I had a secret. Mother said, "We all have burdens to bear." This was my burden to bear, and it was a big one. At times, it would prove almost too much for me to handle.

Life had changed for me again, this time forever, too much, too fast. My big sister had been taken from me, my little brother and sister were not easily accessible all of the time, my parents were practically out of touch from me by letter or by phone, the aunties and uncles were verbally, physically, and to some, even sexually abusive, and the doctors I had trusted were dangerous. I realized that I had no one that would look out for me. I had to take care of myself. I determined that I would be, I must be, a survivor, and I knew, somehow, I would be okay. Because I had to be okay. Things would be different from now on. But I did not know *how* they would differ, or how I would protect myself.

I arrived back at KA late that afternoon. I was thankful when I found out that everyone had already gone to dinner. I told the auntie that I felt sick and needed to stay in the sick room. She allowed me to stay that first night so I wouldn't have to face all the kids. When she brought my pajamas from my room, they didn't fit in the waist, either, and had to be cut on both sides to accommodate the cast. From then on, most all of my clothes had to be cut to allow for the cast. I looked pretty strange, but we were able to salvage most of them five months later when the cast was finally removed. Looking back, I found my spirit and my self-esteem had not been as easy to salvage as my clothes. Fear, distrust, and "going away" were added to loneliness as my daily companions.

During those months that I was in the cast, February to June, I really missed my family. There was a longing and sadness in my heart I could not fill. For the first few weeks, I had to give up those wonderful Sunday afternoon walks. I was not allowed to participate in our Physical Ed classes or do anything strenuous. Instead of showers, I got to take baths in Auntie Harriett's apartment as long as I didn't get the cast wet. I would put about one inch of water in the tub and soak for a few minutes. The privacy was comforting and was one of the best times of my day. During those few minutes, I was alone in my own little world. It was wonderful.

Another good thing about the cast was, I didn't have to sift sand for those few months. One of the uncles placed a piece of plywood under my mattress to keep it from sagging in the middle. This made the thin mattress extra hard, and my bony body had no give against the cast. Sleeping was difficult. Heat rash was a constant problem. Even though I was told not to, I would slide pencils or combs under the cast just to alleviate the painful itching. And I developed bruises and sores. I also tried to hide the cast and even pretend it wasn't there, especially around the boys and staff, because they reminded me of what the man with no face and no hands had done to me. Mother and my Dad knew about my cast, but I wanted to write to them and tell them the details about the awful problems I was having with it. I knew my letters would be read and censored by the aunties so that was not an option as we were not allowed to complain to our parents. That was not doing our part as good missionary kids.

The end of the school year arrived like molasses flowing in January. I was finally going to get out of that cast. I was really dreading having to go back to Jos and see the man with no face, voice, or hands. So I asked our school nurse about it.

"What? No, you don't *have* to go back to Jos to have it taken off. I can cut it off with a little hack saw and a large pair of scissors," she said hesitantly. I was so happy I started jumping around like a chicken on a June bug. That nurse thought I was crazy, and she wasn't far from being right.

Chapter Six

Kano: Hausa Language School

During the following summer, in 1963, my parents were transferred from Lagos to the Hausa Language School in Kano. (See map on page ix.) We left all of the furniture which came with the house. The incoming family would use that furniture until they were transferred, then the next family would use it, and so on. We loaded up our little Hillman Husky, a four-door British-made station wagon, with our meager belongings, and the six of us headed out on the road trip of our lives, the sixth member of our family being, of course, Prince, our miniature dachshund. We were headed for Kano.

Kano is located in the northern part of Nigeria and is the second largest city next to Lagos. The city is populated mostly by the Hausa people, with Islam being their main religion. It is always hot in Kano, averaging in the nineties year round. May through September is the rainy season where it may rain any-where from fifteen to over twenty days a month. During this season, the temperatures are somewhat cooler. On the other hand, the dry season, October through April, may yield no rain at all.

As we were leaving Lagos, my thoughts were again all about Maria. The transition brought back the feelings of that night at the train station as if it had just happened. Saying goodbyes and leaving anything and anyone was difficult for me by now. Leaving my first home in Africa, even if we had only been there for two years, was difficult, and left me in a deep depression. But I sucked in those feelings and settled into the back of the car with the twins. The twins were six now, and I could actually enjoy doing things with them. They were very different from each other. Ann was more quiet and reserved and liked to read. And she loved her animals, especially her dog. Edward was active and loved to work with my Dad and tinker with things. Edward was very sociable and good with his hands. It was only a short time later he built his first working model engine.

Dad had the directions mapped out from Lagos to Kano. We followed a pretty direct route going north through Ibadan, Ogbomosho, Abuja, Kaduna, and then into Kano. Each town that we planned for a stop-over had a missionary station, and since petrol stations were a rare commodity, we mainly tried to hop from one missionary station to another for bathroom breaks or a cool drink. We also bought our petrol, food, and lodging mostly at the mission stations but some off of the local economy as well. The distance from Lagos to Kano was approximately 650 to 700 miles, and my Dad's plan was to make it to Kano in a week. Considering it was the rainy season, and the roads would be washed out, two young kids and a dog needing frequent breaks, and me wanting my Dad to stop and let me take in everything about the African culture I possibly could, the week was quite an adventuresome task.

Our suitcases and boxes were strapped to the top of the car. Mother was in the front seat telling my Dad how to drive. The twins, Prince, and I sat in the back seat. The lack of air-conditioning and dirt roads made breathing difficult. The paved roads had so many potholes and so much surface damage, we bounced all over the place. My Dad said he'd rather have the dirt roads. They were fun at times. Nevertheless, off we went like a herd of turtles.

I thought the journey would be long and boring. Hour after hour, stuck in the back seat with the twins didn't sound like a lot of fun. It turned out I was wrong. Before we had even left the city of Lagos, I threw a barrage of questions to my parents about the things I was seeing. As we drove through the towns and out into the country side, I queried them.

"How do round-a-bouts work?"

"Why do the cars drive on the wrong side of the road?"

"Why are all of the products in the stores different from the products we have in the American stores?"

"Why didn't you carry us on your back instead of using a stroller? It looks so much easier."

Many of these questions my parents couldn't answer. And then there were the questions I couldn't ask, but were always heavy on my heart.

"Why did we have to leave Maria?"

"How can you send all of your children away? Don't you miss us? Don't you love us?"

"Why is it the white people who are always in charge?"

A fascination with travel and learning about the values and customs of the people not only in Africa, but all over the world blossomed in me.

"Why does one country have mostly white people and another country mostly black people?"

"How does that actually happen and why?"

"How did different languages begin?"

The questions tumbled though my young head. I had general ideas before, but I was passionate about learning and talking about these topics as they popped up along the way. It made for a great road trip.

We would rise up early in the morning to avoid the worst of the heat. We'd drive for several hours. Many of the hours were spent driving through the lush bush. My favorite part of the bush was its apparent isolation. I could look out and see an endless horizon of grassland spotted by beautiful three to five hundred-year-old majestic and unique baobab trees. These trees grow to be very tall, and the trunks are very large relative to the branches, which absorb a great deal of water during the rainy season. During the dry season, the tree produces a very nutritious fruit, high in antioxidants. For this reason, it is also called the "Tree of Life."

I was also fascinated by the ant hills that dotted the bush landscape. A deep rust red in color, a fully developed hill standing anywhere between three to seven or eight feet in height and as wide as five or six feet in diameter. Some are rounded like mounds resting on the ground while others have pointed spirals like a makeshift castle rising from the ground. These anthills are created by the ants going underground and digging subterranean

tunnels for the colony. They dig through the dirt and remove it by carrying it to the surface in their mandibles. They then dispose of the dirt near the surface of the opening so that it doesn't fall back. This whole process results in the size, shape and even the composition of the anthill. Ants are fascinating to watch and move more earth than any other creature, even the earthworm!

This is a picture of a huge ant hill. Picture: Courtesy of Kent Academy Archives and Kent Academy Children.

I was constantly asking my Dad to stop the car and take my picture beside the "biggest anthill that ever existed."

Beyond the beautiful scenery, you could begin to see an indication of life in the bush. Small, well-worn paths appeared everywhere once you got right up on them. They were wide enough for only one person, so that if you met some coming on the path, one of you would have to step off until the other passed. These paths usually led to a mud hut or two, but usually no more than four. The dwellings were small with thatched roofs. These Africans had to be as self-sufficient as possible, living on what they grew and the game they could kill. If you were doing all right, you would have owned a goat or two, which supplied your meat and milk. If you were well off, you probably owned a cow or two for the same reasons, in addition to the goat. Of course, if you had a daughter of marrying age, you would also need some animals for the dowry.

One thing my Dad learned to be very cautious about— stopping the car. Since there was no air conditioning, the windows were already down. If we were at a stop sign, hawkers and street beggars would descend on our little car from out of nowhere in a matter of seconds, like flies to a turd. They would push anything from boiled peanuts to bread, toys, and shoes into any window of the car yelling, "I gif you gud price. Ples tek it." They would often drop something in your lap and then say, "Gif me twelf shilling and be done. Iss gud price." Most of the time, we would throw a few six pence or a shilling out of the windows and drive away as soon as possible. They would quickly yell, "Ach, ach, tank you, Sah! Tank you, Madame. God blis you." I felt a little bad about throwing money to distract them, but getting the crowd to chase the money was the only way we could get all of the arms and hands out of the windows so that we could continue our journey.

Occasionally, we would stop along the way at a local market or store advertising *Coco-Cola*. Coke was introduced to Nigeria in 1951 and was heavily advertised throughout Nigeria since it had first been bottled and distributed throughout the regions beyond and into the rural areas. It was still difficult to purchase at the consumer level outside of the major cities when I arrived in 1960, the year the orange drink Fanta was introduced. Fanta seemed to be everywhere from the very start of its introduction. Yet, since my family was from Atlanta, the home of Coca Cola, everywhere we stopped, we had high hopes of getting an ice-cold Coca Cola.

The first thing we learned was that soft drinks were not served cold or with ice. There was a custom then to serve soda at room temperature. I learned that on my first trip to KA. The main reason was because there was no ice, no refrigeration, and most often no electricity. Fanta, another Coca Cola product, was much more accessible, even though it had only been introduced in Nigeria since 1960. It was hip to advertise Coke even when it was not available, which proved most frustrating for my family and any other would-be Coke customer. The false advertisement was effective in bringing in customers. We would eagerly ask for a Coke, and the reply would be, "No Coke, only Fanta." This happened so much across Nigeria that it soon became a saying among the expatriates when something disappointing would happen to you. Whenever you couldn't get something you wanted, you would just say, "No Coke, only Fanta" and that seemed to explain it.

It often related to the inefficiency of the way the country was run. For example, so many times you would try to place a telephone call only to have the operator sleepily say, "De lin is out of orda," and hang up on you. Or, "You must call back tomorrow. Not on seat." And you knew they just didn't want to place the call. If you called back and asked for someone else, there would be no response, or "Sorry, Madame, bye." Sure, everyone gets a little tired from time to time, but in Nigeria "No Coke, Only Fanta" became an accepted way of life.

After Nigeria gained independence from the British in 1960, it suffered growing pains, as any young country would. Unrest sprang up between the major ethnic groups: The Hausas, the Igbos, the Fulanis, and the Yorubas, as each vied for power. If you spoke to the Nigerians, many of them blamed the social unrest and ethnic conflict on the British. This would ultimately lead to a bloody Civil War, AKA, the Biafran War, which started in 1966.

As early as 1960, after Independence Day, the unrest had begun. This unrest would show itself as vehicle searches at various road stops. Often during the searches of the personal belongings and people in the vehicles, the armed soldiers found things of value that they fancied, such as a camera or an American item that could not be obtained in Nigeria. When this happened, they would boldly state with false authority, "Dis must be fo de govenment. I tek it." There was nothing we could do under the circumstances other than give them what they wanted. When a checkpoint official took my Dad's camera, with all of our family pictures on the film, my Dad turned to the rest of us in the car and said, "No Coke, only Fanta." Check-points were scary events for us, and we knew they weren't laughing matters, but I was old enough to know that my Dad didn't want the younger twins, and even me, to live in fear. Mother's response was to have a serious prayer of thanks to the Lord for once more keeping us safe in His arms and safe from all harm. The twins and I would settle back in the back seat and resort to our own ways of coping with the stress this caused, until we would hear my Dad say, "Okay kids, we got another check-point. Stay seated, don't look out of the car window, and don't say anything until we get back out on the road." I learned a lot during those times. By holding my breath, I could slow the rate of my racing heart. I would imagine the worst that might happen and then figure out a way for me and my family to survive. I would be so busy trying to think of a solution I would be oblivious to what was being said by the soldiers or what was going on. I learned to take care of myself and to be strong. I learned resilience.

Simply stated, the Brits left the Nigerians heavily divided among the four ethnic groups, the Igbo in the East; the Fulanies, a nomadic tribe; the Hausa, mostly in the north; and the Yoruba, more in the southern part of Nigeria. The Brits left these groups with no natural ties or governmental structure as to who or how they would rule. The country was also divided by religion, with the Northern part being mostly Muslim and the Southern areas heavily Christian. Riots and conflicts broke out. It affected our trip because in between the cities, along the roads, there were military checkpoints where travelers were stopped. These check-points were frequent and without warning. Sometimes we would catch the guards napping at the check-point station in the heat of the day. We really didn't know whether to wait until they woke up or just continue on our journey. If they caught someone going through the gate, they could and would shoot them.

At times, the soldiers waved us through without so much as looking at us; other times they would menacingly run up to our vehicle waving their guns at us and yell, "Stop, stop dis car!" And we would fear for our lives. Sometimes they would detain us while they methodically went through our luggage, piece by piece. I remember at one stop, they picked up a tampon in Mother's suitcase and made her open it and pull it all apart because they wanted to make sure it wasn't contraband. I felt so sorry for Mother because she was scared, tired, embarrassed, and all of this nonsense made her cry. Rarely does Mother show any signs of weakness, so when I saw her like this, I knew she was at the end of her rope. My anger was at a very high level. But what could I do? The next military stop went easier for us. The guard asked for our papers; my Dad gave them to him for the whole family. He read them and looked at us.

"Oh, you wok for SIM. I go to ya chach (church) in de Oda proveence," he said with a smile on his face. "Pless haf a safe janey and God speed!" And before my Dad could put his papers away, there was a loud pop. My Dad yelled to us to get down in the car. I had already turned in the direction of the pop to see what it was, and as Dad was pulling away from the check point, I saw a guard holding a gun in the car window of someone already slumped over the steering wheel. He had been shot. Why? We'll never know. My guess was that he was an Igbo.

~ ~ ~

On our journey to Kano, we had to be especially careful of the lorries on the roads. These were basically converted large trucks with boards interspersed across the width of the lorry for

the passengers to sit with their backs in the direction they are headed. A lorry driver was considered a fairly respectable job; however, the drivers were not trained in any form or fashion, and most drove like maniacs. Many of the drivers

Motto for this lorry: "Drive Safely."

took the job a little too seriously and took ownership of those small, less than functional roads. We knew to give way when we saw one coming.

Brightly painted and covered with advertisements, especially the passenger lorries, all had nameplates over the front windshield and over the back tag with their own personal sayings. Most of the sayings made no sense to anyone except the owner of the lorry, or to the author of the saying. One example was, "One with God is a majority." I am sure it meant something to that lorry owner. Another one my Dad thought was funny was, "No telephone to heaven."

On our long road trip, and for the rest of the time we were in Africa, we always made a game of reading these signs. One sign, "Peace be to all," was posted on a lorry flying down the center of the road with people hanging out, chickens tied to the sides, someone gripping a goat, and the wheels wobbling precariously. We also passed a lorry named "Drive Safely" which had ended up on the side of the road, totaled. I remember seeing one named "*Jagga, jagga*" and I learned that the words meant "junk" in Hausa. In general, the lorries were lovingly known as "merchants of death" by the Nigerians, and for that reason, we held a healthy respect for them. As our seven-hundred-mile journey progressed, Dad got more and more brazen as his frustration with the lorry drivers increased. If a lorry got too far on our side of the road, he would stick his head out of the window and yell, "Move over, you big pile of junk!" And Mother would say, "Oh, Rolan, hush now."

After six days of driving, we pulled into the SIM compound in Kano, making good time for Nigerian road travel. We looked like a bunch of tramps, but we made it. The little Hillman Husky was truly a pile of junk by now. We warmly named it "Jagga, Jagga," thanking it for getting us to Kano safely. I had just ridden seven hundred miles, windows down, from the southern part to the northern part of Nigeria. I had sucked up every smell, breathed in no telling what, seen many sights, and listened to every sound imaginable along the way. I was totally invigorated by the experience. I had fallen in love with Africa and its people. I felt at home in this country, grateful for the wonderful feelings its people had given me. It was a changing point in my African life.

I loved going into the *kasuwa* (market) along the way to see the beautiful curios made by the Africans. There were traditional African masks, hand carved from ebony wood and polished to a high shine. You could also find carvings of animals and reptiles, and carvings of kitchen necessities such as plates, large spoons and forks, small bowls, and large bowls. Mother found a complete carved nativity scene, complete with baby Jesus that she had to have. Besides the carvings, the beaded jewelry really caught my eye. I still didn't wear much jewelry, but the way the rows of beaded necklaces caught the sun's rays and sparkled so brightly caused me to stop and admire them for several minutes. And my Dad didn't let me leave without one. I liked it even more when I found out how they were made. The children would collect beer bottles, coke bottles, or anything glass; and the artists would melt the glass, color it with dye, and form the colored, molten glass into beads of various simple styles and shapes. Cotton string was used to secure the beads.

Market day—My favorite day of the week.

My favorite markets, though, were the food and fabric markets. The meat section bustled. It opened early in the morning before the heat of the day could turn the meat. Cows, pigs, chickens, horses, and a number of smaller animals I did not even recognize; as well as fish and birds were sold. But I enjoyed watching them cut the meat and display it on rows of long tables. The flies were as thick on the meat as molasses on pancakes. And as Nigerians are a thrifty people, nothing on the animal was wasted, so there were many inviting items laying on the tables, including the hooves, horns, tails, and, uh, well, <u>all</u> parts of the animal were for sale.

To me, the area where they sold the fabric was the most beautiful of the whole market. By now, I'd had two years of sewing at school, and I could make skirts and simple blouses, so I loved to shop for the colorful African prints. I would walk up and down the aisles of the market touching the fabric, taking in the smells, greeting the sellers, and practicing my skills of *chiniki* (bargaining).

Nigerians like to settle everything through compromise, or a give and take process, even down to the marriage arrangement. In the market there are no price tags, yet everything has a price. The process of *chiniki*, is the buyer and seller determining a mutually agreed upon price for a desired purchase. In the market, if you do not *chiniki*, it is considered rude, as it appears to the seller that you don't value his or her wares. The process may go something like this:

"Sannu da zuwa," (Hello) says the buyer. "My friend, how much for this basket?"

"Yauwa, Sannu," (Hello to you as well) says the seller. "De baskit iss twelf shilling, no less." You, the buyer, knowing that it is custom to *chiniki*, know that he will tell you a price over the fair price. And so you will offer just a little under what he offers as well as a little under fair market price. So you will say,

"Ach, ach. My friend, you try to rob me? I will gif you nine shilling in gud faith." I always spoke to them in broken English. It was fun, and if I did it respectfully, I used it as a way to put us on the same level.

"No, no, Madame. Diss will not do. Ples, I haf family to feed. Pay me levan shilling, I pray." This continues until both parties agree on ten shillings, which was the fair market price all along.

I loved to *chiniki*. The more the item was valued or desired, the further apart in price the bargaining would start. It was fun, and the Africans love to see a young white girl do it. We would laugh and laugh, and then I would end up giving them a dash (tip) in the end just because we had a good time.

My stay in Kano would last only one summer. We would only be in Kano for six months, we were assigned to one large guest room for the whole family, including Prince, our dog. Our room had a bathroom with a cement tub (which took some getting used to), a double bed for Mother and Dad (two twin beds pushed together), a single twin bed for me, and an army bunk bed for the twins. My parents' job was to learn the Hausa language during their six-month stay in Kano, so they each had a desk for studying. The twins and my jobs were to essentially stay out of their way and take care of Prince. Believe me, I was getting pretty good at staying out of my parents' way. But we had to really keep our eyes on Prince. The Africans from the bush would not hesitate to grab Prince for chop-chop. We ate our meals in the Big House, family-style, and just as in Lagos, we were invited around to the missionaries' homes for dinner to get acquainted with the SIM family. When I first arrived in Africa, I hated those meals. I was so shy, I didn't know how to act or what to say, especially if they weren't Americans. But after some time, I began to look forward to them. I wanted to learn about their cultures, eat their food, hear their languages, absorb everything I could that was different.

Most SIM compounds were similar in composition. They were tight knit with strong security. On the larger compounds, like Kano, there was a Big House, where the missionaries gathered for meals, meetings, and other public gatherings. It was usually in the center of the compound. Clustered around the Big House were some of the business buildings, like a post office for the convenience of the missionaries, meeting/classrooms, the clinic, and the BD (known as the Business Department). Many times the BD included a mini grocery store for the convenience of the bush missionaries. Further out were the guest rooms for the missionaries like us who were there for various reasons, and had come in for supplies or stopovers, or language school. Contributing to the independence of the mission, there were also a chapel and in Kano, the famous eye hospital.

Here, like in Lagos, we met missionaries from all over the world. I liked that, and I promised myself that one day I would visit all of these interesting countries. I made friends with one couple from Alaska. They proudly told us how beautiful their state was and how they liked the beautiful mountains and glaciers. I put Alaska at the top of my list to visit. Little did I know I would go twice to Alaska someday, as well as many other countries around the world, fifty-three countries to be exact.

When I came back to our room each night, I fell asleep to the delicious, yet pungent odor of roasting groundnuts, or peanuts, in the air. A quarter mile down the street from our little cottage was one of the largest peanut factories in Nigeria. The factory processed peanuts and peanut oil, one of the largest exports of northern Nigeria at the time. Once the peanuts were processed and ready for export, they were stacked in these huge pyramids. Mother and my Dad had given me a bike for this past Christmas. I used to ride it down the road from the mission, and watch the employees carry the big, heavy, and from what I could perceive, burlap bags on their heads up a ramp onto the heap while precisely building the pyramid. These pyramids were said to be composed of as many as 15,000 bags each. In fact, it was such an accomplishment when a pyramid was completed that everyone around would stop what they were doing to go watch the last bag being placed on the very top. French West Africa and British West Africa were second to India alone in the groundnut producing industries of the world during Nigeria's pre-independence years.

The sound of African High Life, the local pop music, was prevalent in the area's local bars and open-air restaurants. One could also hear beating drums in the distance. I felt so content with the sounds and smells of Africa, and I slept well even though I was conscious of the fact that summer was passing quickly. Soon I would be going back to school, that place where I always seemed to lose myself.

~ ~ ~

While living in Kano, I got to experience a fascinating African rite of passage. The Fulani tribe, the mostly nomadic tribe who follows their cattle in northern Nigeria, required all of their young men to go through "the Fulani beatings," their initiation rites into manhood. Passing the initiation allowed the young men all the benefits and privileges of the men in the village. Later in life, I would do research on these initiations rites. I discovered that the government had come to look down on bodily markings and heavy beatings, resulting in the easing up of these rituals. But when I lived in Nigeria, they were prevalent, and I witnessed them firsthand.

My Dad and I were invited to visit a village about an hour and a half outside of Kano by Mr. Peterson, an SIM missionary who lived in Kano. Mr. Peterson was the epitome of a stereotypical British-born missionary in Africa. He wore an old, grungy pith helmet, a khaki shirt, and very baggy white shorts. He kept calling me "Muffin," and he was hard of hearing, so every time you said something to him he would reply, "Eh, *Whot?*" I thought he was hilarious and was excited to get to go on an excursion with just him and Dad. He had explained to us what the ritual was all about so Mother decided the twins should stay behind. In fact, Mother didn't think I should go either, but I begged so hard that Dad finally said, "Aw, Momma, let the child go. She'll learn something." It wasn't an easy sell, but she eventually relented.

Mr. Peterson drove in an old Land Rover, and the trip took us about an hour. We passed through the ancient city of Kano, built between 1095 AD through 1134 AD, and completed mid-fourteenth century. The city is surrounded by a wall built of mud. The wall's estimated original height was thirty to fifty feet high and about forty feet thick at the base. It has about fifteen gates scattered around it and was built to protect the citizens who lived inside. I was told that only Muslims were allowed inside the walled city, no whites, and no one of non-Muslim faith. I loved passing by the ancient city because it was such a mystery. I used to think of ways that I could get in, to be the only non-Muslim to have penetrated the gates.

Just past the ancient city, the road became very narrow, and what little smooth pavement there was had disappeared. I was grateful we were in the Land Rover as it was well-suited for the rough roads. We were getting into the bush now. The little shacks with tin roofs turned to mud huts with straw tops, but they were as scarce as hen's teeth. It was the rainy season, so the air was hot and heavy. I hung out of the back seat window like a blubbering dog. I could smell rain in the air, and although I loved nothing more than a good afternoon African rain shower, I hoped it wouldn't rain that particular day.

After about a half-hour of driving, the road ended, and we came to a grove of trees. Mr. Peterson stopped the vehicle. By this time the road had turned into a wide path. My heart started pound-ing, and I was full of excitement.

"They know me well and don't pay me any mind," Mr. Peterson told us. "But I have never brought anyone with me. So I am going to ask you to stay back at first to see how they react. If they are fine with your presence, then I will bring you closer." He raised his voiced, and finished by saying, "And, by George, stay together!! These things can get quite hairy!" Dad and I looked at each other, wide eyed, as we wondered what we were getting into.

We got out of the Land Rover and walked down a narrower path through some trees towards the village. I could hear drums beating and men singing. It was such a moving sound. The drum beat seemed to reverberate inside of me, and I felt my body yearning to move with the music. As we came closer, I caught a glimpse through the trees of the people moving in unison in a clearing. Finally, as we got to the clearing, Mr. Peterson led us over to a spot near the back of the crowd.

"Stay here," he said firmly, as he strode off into the explosive crowd.

Dad and I didn't have a chance to ask a question or say a word. As we watched Mr. Peterson walk away, we looked at each other and grinned, knowing we were in for something extraordinary. We were surrounded by boys and men; there was not a woman or girl in sight. I knew they must be somewhere around because I could smell something delicious in the air, but being the only girl in the immediate location caused me to feel self-conscious. I was glad Mother let me wear long pants that day instead of the dresses she usually insisted on. Dad had told me to tuck my hair up as well, so I wrapped it into a knot on the top of my head, and covered it with my hat.

Mr. Peterson was gone about twenty minutes, but it seemed like an hour to me. Finally, we saw him making his way back through the crowd. He told us there were four young men to be initiated into manhood and then to be married. He gave us permission to watch from a closer vantage point. The three of us made our way slowly and tentatively through the crowd closer to the center until it was safe. The action was taking place at the center of the circle made by the men and boys of the village. A young boy with white markings on his face, wearing a brightly colored loincloth and arm bracelets on his upper arm was holding a mirror. I loudly whispered a question to Mr. Peterson as to the purpose of the mirror, and he responded that the young man was to hold it up to his face while being beaten. If he showed any kind of pain or discomfort, he would be humiliated and not accepted into manhood by the elders and his peers. Then, at a later time chosen by the elders, he may be allowed to go through the ordeal again.

By this point, many of the celebrations had gotten underway, and many of the men and elders of the village were drunk on palm wine. A couple of older men stood beside the initiate. Suddenly, the circle expanded. It surprised me, just about knocking me down. I managed to stay on my feet, though, and looked back in the center of the circle. The beating of the drums intensified, the singing stopped, and a man dressed in feathers and painted lavishly ran out into the circle waving a long stick. He was yelling and speaking in Fulani.

~ ~ ~

During these rushes, Dad and I would lose each other for a time. With each rush, I panicked because I couldn't see over the crowd. I would bend down to look under the crowd until I spotted the familiar skinny white legs and baggy white shorts of Mr. Peterson. Relieved, I would work my way over to him, and together we'd find Dad.

The ritual itself was quite stunning. The man in feathers would dance around the initiate still waving his long stick high in the air. Then he would stop in front of the initiate and bring the stick down and right across the initiate's chest. This would happen two to four times. Every time the soft flesh of the young man's chest was hit, his skin swelled up and popped open. The sound was akin to a branch cracking in half. I was amazed as I watched the boy's face. He did not flinch or even blink. No reaction at all. After the strikes, the wounds were quickly filled with warm white ash from a pot kept near the fire located in the center of the circle. This would cause the scars to enlarge and turn black as they healed. The boy would wear the resulting scars with pride as they were considered beautiful in the eyes of women and seen as a sign of courage and manhood to the men.

This day, the young man passed his initiation rite into manhood, as the vast majority did. The crowd's exhilaration was contagious, and the exotic smell of their sweaty bodies lent an authenticity to the adventure. I couldn't believe it. I had seen a native Fulani successfully achieve the rite of passage from boy to man.

The Fulani beatings.

This was the Africa of which I loved being a part. It was the most real, raw emotion I had ever experienced. I felt sad for the boy's pain, but I shared his pride as I watched the men help him walk away—a man now in his culture. I laughed with glee at the wonder of what I had just experienced, knowing he would celebrate with food and then choose his bride. My Dad looked over at me. A large warm smile spread across his face. I think he understood what I was feeling completely because he was feeling it, too. That day was a day I would remember for the rest of my life!

"Eh, Chap," Mr. Peterson began, "and Muffin, let's not press our luck. We'd best be going before the rains start." As badly as I wanted to stay, I stepped in line behind him. He took us out of the village on a different path, a path which led us right through the women's section.

While the men were busy with the rites of passage, the women had been preparing delicious, fragrant food. The Fulani were a poor, nomadic tribe, who followed their cattle, so I am not sure what meat they had at this celebration. They often ate goat or dog, but on very special occasions they might sacrifice one of their precious cows. Yams, corn, and a wheat bean cake with peppers were also served. I loved the bean cakes and used to eat them every chance I could. It was a simple meal batter which was drop fried and except for the red hot pepper inside, was very similar to our southern hush puppies. The girls who were ready for marriage were also here. They were dressed in their brightest colored zanies and wraps and kept hidden for the wedding ceremonies to come. I wished we could have stayed to watch the selection process and then the weddings take place, but unfortunately the rains were coming and Mr. Peterson said directly to my Dad that the rest of the ceremonies could get "quite frisky, if you know what I mean, old chap?" Then he gave a laugh that sounded a little too frisky to me if you know what I mean. Eh, Whot!

That night as I lay in bed with pleasant thoughts swirling, I was full of emotion. I had been privileged to experience the culture of this Fulani extended family, a ritual that reflected their personal values, a special private family event, and I felt special. I would never be the same because of what all I had experienced this day because of what one Fulani village shared with me.

Meditation on Loving Kindness

*May all beings live with death over their left shoulder, and
kindness in the center of their heart.
May all beings be free of suffering. May all beings know
the great
good fortune of their great nature.
May all beings be at peace.*

— Meditation by Stephen Levine

Chapter Seven

Kano: My Friend, the Leper

It was a Saturday, sometime during summer break. Usually, I would stay around the guest room and read books, my new favorite pastime, but my parents were studying for a Hausa exam and wanted the twins and me outside. Sara, my best and only friend at the Kano mission, was nowhere to be found that day, so I was alone to do my own bidding. I knew there were lots of sights to see and places to explore outside of the mission, especially at the market, so I decided to ride my bike there. I was still excited from seeing the initiation rites and was in an adventurous spirit.

The Kano market was an exciting and sometimes frightening place to be. It was in a constant state of motion, day and night. The crowd's ebb and flow felt like waves hitting you with force, and you emerged in a current of people, as you gently drifted on down the rows of market goods. In a world of dirt floors, mud walls, or *zana* (straw mat walls), and tin roofs that made a deafening noise when it rained, color reigned supreme. The Nigerians enjoy bright color, and especially in the market, you didn't just see the color; you felt it. Stall after stall of cooking pots featured vibrant, bold colors that I'd never seen matched together back in the States.

Rows of multicolored fabric stretched on for miles. There were stalls of tie-dyed materials that would be made into the *zane* (rhymes with Connie) that were meticulously wrapped around the bodies of the women. And the contrasting *goyo* (rhymes with yoyo) cloth held their babies close to their backs. Carefully wrapped pads helped to distribute the weight carried on the women's heads to make balance easier for their heavy loads.

Even though I had seen it hundreds of times before, I watched with admiration as a young female shopper, balancing a load of wares on her head, sometimes up to two or three times the size of her baby, with more ease than I could balance on my bicycle, stopped to give her baby a refreshing drink. Without removing the load on her head, the mother swiftly untied her goyo, and using her hip as a support, slid the baby around to her front. With one arm holding the baby, the mother reached close to the ground with her free hand and cupped a drink from a faucet of running water. The happy child drank from her hand until satisfied. Then, with one upward thrust and twist of her hips, the child was again resting safely on the mother's back. I imagined it must have been a wonderful feeling to have another human so close to my body in such an innocent and loving, protective way. It contrasted with my feelings of separation and loneliness from my family, from my sister, Maria, and yes, even from Mother.

The old market was huge, and I knew I could easily get lost; but on that day I ventured into an area where some new stalls were being built. These stalls weren't put together by shingles propped up by loose rocks or whatever else could be found lying about like the older ones. Their modern structure made them look out of place. These were new, modern stalls, maybe seven feet wide, with poured cement floors and cinder block walls up to maybe six feet tall on all three sides. There were about ten or twelve of them in a row still in the process of being built.

I walked along each one of them, throwing small stones at the lizards that had become trapped within the walls. I also wondered how the poor lizards would ever get out once they had cornered themselves.

Lizards are everywhere in Nigeria, as common as squirrels in Georgia. I remembered how they used to frighten me when I first came to Nigeria, but then I learned that they were just as frightened of me as I was of them. It got to the point where I stopped even noticing them. Lizards provide an ecological balance in the country relative to the ants and insects, which is their main diet. They would run in the yards, through the house, hide in my shoes, and generally be in sight at all times. In the market, the bright orange heads, reddish tails and black bodies of the males made them particularly easy to spot, especially against the white cement structure of the new stalls. The poor lizards were not used to such stalls where there were no small holes through which they could run and steal a small morsel of food, escaping unnoticed.

My timing was perfect. Just as the tropical sun was beginning to set, I made it to the last few stalls. A few of the market vendors were packing their wares for the night. I spied a lizard doing pushups on the top of the wall. I slowly reached down to pick up a small stone, while at the same time thinking it was time for me to head back. My hand was about four inches from the stone when I heard a continuous, soft low moan, a moan that seemed to vibrate somewhere inside me. My body froze. That sound, unlike any sound I had ever heard in my thirteen years of life, couldn't be human. But it wasn't an animal either. It was a sound that would haunt me for a long time to come.

Although I didn't know it at that moment, it was the sound of someone dying. It felt as if the sound was made for the purpose of reassuring the maker that there was still life; still enough dignity and control to master even the simplest of human function. I was drawn to it in spite of myself. As I rounded the wall opening into the last stall, my eyes took a moment to adjust from the intensity of the setting sun. The soft wail was coming from the corner of the stall, from a mound of filthy rags. Thinking it might possibly be a wounded animal, I slowly approached the form. When I was about five feet away, a head slowly raised. My heart jumped. I dropped to my knees, unable to run away, unable to utter a sound of my own; I was horrified.

It was a man. His nose had been eaten away, leaving only an open sore in the middle of his anguished face. His top lip was also gone, showing below it a knotty purplish gum. I could see no teeth. His mouth moved in a contorted manner. He had no hands to reach out for help, just stubs at the ends of his arms. Both legs were gone at the knees. Upon closer inspection, he had only one ear, and the other side of his head was a mass of open sores. I remember thinking that with only one ear, maybe he would be less able to hear some of the hatred, prejudice, and lack of compassion that had placed him here.

This man was an untouchable, a leper. I had no way of knowing his story, but I did know of the ostracism and the banishment of people of his kind. In that moment, I felt anger towards the God I had been raised to respect and love for what he had allowed to happen to one of his own creatures. I felt compassion for this suffering, dying man.

Why was there sadness and loneliness in this world? Where was this Jesus who was supposed to love and care for his creatures, big and small? And in that visit with my friend, the leper, I lost my childhood concept of God. The image of a benevolent white man with long white hair and a beard with children gathering at his feet was forevermore a fake to me. My off-and-on anger at God was now in full swing. My confusion as to why God allowed bad things to happen to good people turned to revulsion. I didn't want anything to do with God, Jesus, or Lord anymore. My child heart had felt more anguish and pain that I simply could not understand within the context of the loving God I had been brought up to worship. I had heard of him, but as of yet, I had not experienced him except in the negative.

The dying man's eyes never left mine. He was a human being, what was left of one. His lament continued, more like sobs, softer now, squeezing my heart.

Do something for him, Cheryl. Do anything; just do something. Don't just stand there and stare! I told myself. Tears rolled down my cheeks; and I was tormented by my own selfish thoughts. If I didn't get home before dark, there would be trouble with Mother. It could be dangerous for me to make my way home alone in the dark. But there I stood, and there he lay, both of us still staring into each other's eyes.

"What can I do?" I asked aloud. I don't know if he didn't hear me or couldn't understand me, but there was no response. Maybe he had just given up. I couldn't let myself believe that he might be dying.

My parents had given me a few lectures on leprosy when we first arrived in Africa, mainly because I was used to going barefoot in Georgia. In fact, during the summer, it was hard to get a pair of shoes on me. I wanted to continue that delightful habit when I arrived in Africa, but my parents were quick to inform me about the dangers of snakes, army ants, scorpions, and leprosy.

Leprosy is a relatively rare disease caused by the bacteria called mycobacterium leprae, and is a mildly contagious disease. It may take anywhere from six months to forty years to present itself in an individual, and that is usually after repeated contact with an infected individual. It is transmitted between individuals through nose or mouth droplets, or through contact with open sores. The sores usually start with the extremities: fingers, toes, ears, and nose. If left untreated, it spreads to hands and feet, and then to the limbs or face. It literally eats the body. The disease is now treated with antibiotics and can be cured if caught early enough. Examples:

A Fulani woman holding up her badly deformed hand caused by leprosy.

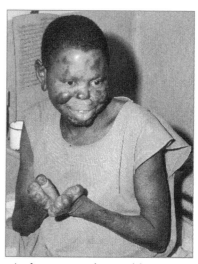

A leprosy patient with severe facial damage. Her hands are all but gone, and she has open sores on her legs.

As the *baba* (old man) continued to hold my gaze, I realized that I was close enough to hear him breathing. I was so drawn in that I didn't notice the stench of rotting flesh and the sound of swarming flies. I was seeing something in this man's eyes that I willed myself never to forget. I saw compassion. I saw pain. I saw determination. I felt a kind of love I had never experienced.

I squatted down, and we sat there together, communicating silently. No words were possible and none needed. I wondered if he knew I could feel the desperation of his plight. But the strongest feeling I had for my leper friend was a deep sense of compassion. I wanted to take his broken body into my arms and protect him from the world and the God that had allowed this to happen. Instead, I stood up, and through my tears told him in a language he probably could not understand, "I love you." I turned and walked into the evening, my young heart laden with guilt and regret.

I never saw him again. Sundays are very busy days at the mission, full of worship, pretense, and self-importance. So the following morning, Monday, while Mother and my Dad were in classes, I went back to the very same spot. My friend was gone; the stench of his rotting body and the buzz of the swarming flies no longer filled the stall. All that remained were some of the rags. I sat down close to where my leper friend had lain. I didn't pray for him because who would hear? Surely not the God who'd left him there in the first place. So I simply talked to him.

I told him about my angry feelings toward God, towards some of the people in my life; and I apologized and asked his forgiveness of me, my parents, and the other missionaries who hadn't reached him in time. I wished him relief from his agony through death if he wished. Then I left. I checked the closest hospital around. It was, of course, the Sudan Interior Mission Eye Hospital (SIM). I did not find him there. I continued, however, to be troubled by my questions: *What happened to him? Did he die? Did someone find him in that god-forsaken stall and take him to the government hospital? Did someone care for and love him in the end? Or did they take him for dead and just dump him somewhere?* I tumbled these questions over and over in my mind. I never received any answers. I never forgot him. And I never shared the encounter with my parents, or anyone else.

~ ~ ~

A few weeks after my encounter with the leper, I had an opportunity of a different kind. The mission had built an eye hospital in the 1940s to take care of the needs of the many lepers in Nigeria, but the hospital had grown to encompass the needs of a greater population, including those who needed surgeries, such as those for cataracts and glaucoma.

During this time, Mother was constantly talking to me about studying nursing, and returning to Africa as a missionary nurse after graduation. But being a missionary was the furthest thing from my mind. I was, however, fascinated with medicine. I even talked with my parents about becoming a doctor. Mother tried to discourage that thought, being uncommon for women at the time.

"Women are just not able to meet the demands that are required of doctors. Women are much more suited to nursing because they are naturally more nurturing," she would explain. She had always wanted to be a nurse but circumstances in her life never allowed it. Still, she never missed a chance to tell Maria and me what a wonderful career nursing would be for us. If her wishes had come true, Maria and I surely would have grown up to be missionary nurses serving in Africa.

Even so, living in Africa sparked my interest in medicine. It gave us privileges that few kids in America would ever receive. I was allowed opportunities to go into the operating rooms and watch the doctors and nurses perform different types of surgeries.

Our mission hospital, the SIM Hospital, was considered one of the most respected places to receive medical care, but even at that, it was a far cry from the US standards. The wards were long and crowded, with beds closely positioned next to each other and no curtains between them for privacy. A constant gentle breeze flowed through the ward from the open windows on both sides, and families brought the meals in for their loved ones. Still in all, it was definitely the place to be if you needed good medical care.

Just before I had to leave to go back to KA, there was one very special eye surgery that had been scheduled at the SIM Eye Hospital in Kano. Plans and arrangements had been going on for months in preparation for this particular surgery. The eye surgeon, whose work I was able to observe, was from Atlanta, Georgia. Dr. Lester had volunteered a few months of his time to work at the Kano Eye Hospital. The patient who had been select-ed for this special surgery was a young blind girl about my same age. Dr. Lester explained to me that this young blind patient, with the donation of a pair of compatible human eyes and a successful operation, would be able to see for the first time with corrective lenses. All we had to do was wait for the compatible eyes, which had finally been found in the United States and flown by TWA into Kano. We didn't have to wait very long—only a few weeks. Dr. Lester would perform the surgery, and I was allowed to watch along with my parents and other missionaries who were interested.

On the day of the surgery, I stood in the hot (again no air conditioning), crowded operating room watching and listening to the doctor's every word as he not only showed us but also explained step-by-step what he was doing. On a nearby table, in a yellow and red thermos container, two eyes stared sightlessly packed in ice. A sticker that read "HUMAN EYES" was wrapped around the canister. I shuddered as the nurses opened it to prepare the two small organs for surgery.

I later learned that the first complete human eye transplant would not be performed in Africa until 1969, but operations using parts of the eye, such as the cornea, were becoming more common in Nigeria in the sixties. Our young friend received a corneal transplant from an unknown donor in the US. The surgery lasted no longer than forty-five minutes. The young girl's head was wrapped in bandages and she was sent on her way to the ward.

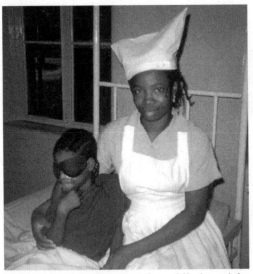

The young girl who went from blind to sight after a simple, yet expensive, surgery.

Sometime later, I was lucky enough to be there when they removed the girl's bandages, as were her parents, the nurses, the chaplain, my Dad and mother, and some of the missionaries from the compound. I squirmed my way through the crowd to get close enough to see what was going on. Dr. Lester slowly unwrapped the bandages, and explained that she would only see blurred images for the first couple of weeks and even after that, she would wear thick glasses.

Then the moment came. At first, a look of confusion appeared on her face, and then pure joy spread slowly across her small, beautiful ebony face. With the help of an interpreter, she tried to explain what it was like to see for the first time, her words tumbling out one after the other so fast her interpreter was useless. She was crying. Her mother and father were crying. And so was I. This experience by itself was enough to make anyone want to go into medicine.

Chapter Eight

The Glass Giraffe

"Kennedy's been shot." Someone yelled in a muffled voice off in the distance.

"Is that Linda running over here?" Amber asked. "What is she saying?"

"Kennedy is dead. Somebody shot him!" Linda approached the window of the room Amber and I shared with two other girls, JoAnn and Ruth. JoAnn turned to me and whispered, "Who is Kennedy, and why is Linda crying?"

The four of us were hanging out of the open windows of our room, eager with anticipation but feeling more confused. I cupped my hand to JoAnn's ear. "Don't bother me with that now. I can't think. I just want to know where my parents are going to be transferred. I'm really worried about it."

A few times a year, the mission held meetings at various compounds to inform the missionaries of recent changes, transfers, and other updates occurring within the mission. One such meeting was happening at the Miango Rest Home next door to KA. One night early in November in my eighth grade year at KA, the announcement would be made as to where my parents would be stationed now that they had successfully completed language school.

Linda, whose parents were on their annual vacation at the Rest Home, didn't have to adhere to KA rules, as she was staying with her parents and had more liberties than the students staying in the dorms. So I asked her to stay at the meeting just long enough to get the news about my parents' transfer and then run over to our dorm room window to let me know. We'd started to worry when she hadn't arrived by nightfall. The fact that it was now dark meant *my guardi*, the night watchman, would be out doing his rounds. If he saw us all talking to Linda out of our windows, there would be some serious sand sifting. By the time she arrived, it was just after 8:30 p.m., after lights out, and the news she had was that someone named John F. Kennedy had been shot. She had no news of my parents' transfer. With a lot of begging and pleading from me, she went back to the meeting to wait until she got the information about my parents.

I was frustrated, but at least I had a few moments to collect my thoughts. Our conversation returned to John F. Kennedy as if to get our minds off the subject at hand.

"John Kennedy. He is the President of the United States of America," I said in response to JoAnn's question of several minutes back.

"Who will be President now?" asked Ruth.

"That would be the Vice President, Johnson, I think," I responded. If we sounded a bit disinterested about the whole shooting incident, it's because we probably were. Living six thousand miles away, American politics were rarely, if ever, discussed. In our classrooms, we had many kids from other countries, and to be fair, we would discuss the political and governmental systems of all countries represented in the class. American celebrities were another group that we did not follow. So when I came back to the States for furlough and didn't know who the TV celebrities or the popular TV programs were, people looked at me like I was an alien.

About fifteen minutes later, after asking Linda to find out more information about my parents, she popped up at the window and scared us all half to death. All four of us screamed. We knew it was a matter of time before an auntie on night duty came down the hall and caught us, so Linda quickly gave me the news.

"Your parents are going to Chanchaga, a leprosarium, for one year, and then they will be transferred to KA for the six months before you go on furlough back to the States. Bye, I've got to get back home before *my guardi* catches me!" With that, she turned and ran back towards her cottage.

"What? Wait! KA? They can't be dorm parents! There must be some mistake!" I hung out the window yelling to Linda just as Auntie June came into the room.

"Girls, girls, girls! What is going on here? Stop all this noise immediately!" By that time, I was crying. To live at a leprosarium was one thing, but to have your parents living at the same school and working in the same dorm as you lived in, that was too much to take in. I had gotten over some of the loneliness I experienced the first two years I was at KA. But kids can be awfully hard on dorm parents, and I didn't want the kids talking about my parents the way we talked about a lot of the other aunties and uncles. It was about the worst thing I could think of. Hypocritical? Yes, but that is just the way it was in boarding school life.

As I scrambled back in bed, JoAnn told Auntie June about my parents being transferred and about the president being shot. Auntie June said she didn't believe the part about the President, but she would check on it in the morning. She made sure we were all in bed while chiding me. "It won't be bad to have your parents here," she said. "Stop being so silly." But she told us goodnight and didn't punish us which was a relief.

After everything quieted down and everyone else was asleep, I was lost in my own thoughts. Christmas holidays were around the corner. It would be good to be with my family again even though we would still be missing Maria. Would that help fill that constant hole in me? Or would it make it worse? In addition, I would be flying to yet another new house, house number four in three years. I would just have to wait and see. *No Coke, Only Fanta,* I thought before I fell asleep.

I remembered our first Christmas in Lagos; we went to a British department store and saw Santa Claus there. Following the British system, Santa Claus was called "Father Christmas." We waited in line so my little brother and sister could go up and sit on his lap, but as soon as we got within seeing distance of him, we saw that he was an African man. He was dressed in the traditional Western costume, complete with very fake-looking white hair, and a long white beard and white mustache that hung off his face. When the twins saw him, they burst into tears and Mother snickered. I could understand the three-year-old twins being a little surprised and afraid, but I became angry at Mother. I didn't have the nerve to tell her the reason for my anger, but I felt she had no right to laugh at the Africans for celebrating Christmas in whatever fashion they wanted. Needless to say, no pictures were taken with Santa that year!

Christmas was a special time at KA. The staff at KA went all out to give us kids a wonderful Christmas. Everything that could be decorated was decorated—the living room, the dining room, the classrooms, and the dormitories. We had a big green tree in the main living room, and each student had his or her own personal filled stocking hung over the fireplace. Try to imagine close to two hundred stockings on one fireplace. Each stocking was filled with candy and gifts that were age and gender appropriate. To be sure, they were small gifts, but nice ones and well thought

out. One year, I received a travel manicure set and a miniature glass animal I dearly loved. It was a clear glass giraffe about two inches tall and three-fourths of an inch wide, wrapped in tissue and nestled in a little gift box. The giraffe had orange and black stripes painted on it with glossy paint, and its slender legs were so fragile. I had to take good care of

Courtesy of Craig Photos

This is the fireplace at Kent Academy where the two hundred or so stockings were hung on the one fireplace.

it so it wouldn't break. I was so proud of that giraffe. To me it said, "You are now and forever a part of Africa."

Each year, we had our annual Christmas party with the staff doing skits and one of the teachers playing Father Christmas. Usually, the senior-most male students would pass out the stockings while some staff members were available to help the younger ones unwrap and manage their new gifts. It was, indeed, a grand party! But the highlight of every year was that Aunt Linda, our dietician and chef, would create a Christmas Wonderland made completely of candy, sugar frosting, and gingerbread. It was set with a gingerbread house, gingerbread people, a sleigh, and frosting snow everywhere. Every year we couldn't wait to see what the wonderland would look like that year. The best part, though, was the kids who flew home the last couple of days got to eat it. It was almost worth flying home last just to get a bite of that frosting snow.

At Christmas, even the staff seemed to relax and become nicer. I guess it was hard on them as well, being away from their homes and families stateside. Everything was different here, so we all tried to make it work. It was ninety-eight degrees outside; our families were thousands of miles away; there was none of the hustle and bustle crowds of Christmas shoppers that I remembered from my American Christmases. Nonetheless, Christmas is probably the best memory I have of KA.

I experienced a lot of new feelings and emotions in eighth grade. In addition to the strong maternal feelings I had for my brother and sister, that same year I also started to take an interest in boys. I'd had a childish fancy for a boy before, but this was different. I really fell for a boy in eighth grade. I had feelings for this boy I had never had before, so I guess you could say he was my first crush. He was the shortest boy in our class. I was the shortest girl in our class. We had that in common. We were also both a little shy. I thought him to be very nice and not mean like a lot of the other boys. I went the first part of the year keeping my feelings to myself. I never told him or any of my friends or roommates how I felt about him although he did catch me looking at him a little longer than anyone else.

After Christmas holiday, he sat next to me in study hall one time, and I was so excited. I felt so warm and happy that someone cared for me in such a way. I wondered if this was what it was like to have a boyfriend. I also knew boyfriends were not really encouraged at the boarding school, but that was not really on my mind at the time. I thought it brave of him to sit next to me so openly. The other boys in the class thought otherwise and teased him mercilessly for days after. He never got up the courage to sit with me again, nor did our relationship advance any further. I was heartbroken. But we did remain secret friends, at least on my end. It wasn't that we had a real boyfriend/ girlfriend relationship, or even that we spent time together, it was just having someone to think about as my own special friend. That was enough to help the lonely afternoons and nights pass and it was a good time for me to have even that one-sided connection.

Chapter Nine

Tears and Laughter in Chanchaga

My parents were transferred to Chanchaga, a small village in the bush centrally located in Nigeria, right before Christmas in 1964, when I was still thirteen years old. The station was the location of our mission leprosarium. My parents moved there while I was away during eighth grade, my third year at KA. This would be my fourth place of residence in as many years, not counting boarding school. There were still boxes all over the house when I arrived from school. My temporary home was on a beautiful compound with a large grassy lawn and widespread acacia trees. The sweet-smelling bright red blooms of the hibiscus bushes along the front of the house penetrated through the dust in the air. The dust was from the harmattan, winds which blow across West Africa during the months of November through March. They come and go like clockwork, and so it is essentially considered a season. The harmattan winds are dry and dusty and originate from the Sahara Desert. They blow through the houses and buildings, leaving a film of dust on everything. The dust cracks your skin and lips and most people cover their faces when going out in the winds.

In addition to the leprosarium, there were only three missionary homes on the compound. My Dad was to assist the station manager in the upkeep of the compound. Sometimes God calls you out to be a missionary printer as he did my Dad, but the mission might have other plans for you. We were pretty much isolated from other people at this station as it was located in a remote area in the bush, but our house was a rather attractive house as far as African homes go. It was a three-bedroom stone house with a large veranda on the front. It had a lightly wooded front yard, and my Dad loved to sit on the veranda in the rocking chairs. He kept his gun handy to shoot dove, or the occasional wild guineafowl which Musa, our cook, would prepare for the evening meal.

The house had a tin roof that made a wonderful thunderous sound when it rained; and it rained to a fault during the rainy season. Nothing compares to the smell and sound of an African rain. I would lie in bed under my new mosquito net and listen to the rains approach from way off in the distance. First, it would gently thunder, then big drops would hit the soft sandy earth as the rains gathered momentum. The closer the rains got, the muskier the smell, a mixture of fresh air and dirt. It was intoxicating. It reached my tin roof hesitantly, just a few drops at a time. One, three, five. Two... ten, fifteen. Then, as if the clouds could hold back no longer, they released their precious load, and the pounding lulled me to sleep. Once again, like my own, I

found myself covered in the tears of Africa.

I had a room to myself, with a chest for my clothes, a chair, and a beautiful white mosquito net over my bed. Most of them were old and of a dingy yellow color. But mine must have been new. It was bright white. When the sun shone on it through the window, it was sparkly. So pretty. Right outside

An approaching storm from behind a missionary's home.

my window, I could watch the acacia trees sway in the breeze as I took my siestas. When I arrived on Christmas break, I could tell this was going to be better than the small one-room apartment we had in Kano while Mother and Dad were in language school.

We had a huge wood stove at our bush home in Chanchaga, and I learned to make delicious yeast bread in the old wood-fired oven. We had no electricity at the station other than a generator for a couple of hours a day. Any ironing we needed to do was done with a kerosene iron. Our ice was made in a small kerosene fridge. For a warm shower, we heated water from a *guaria*, a ten-gallon container that hung on the outside of the bathroom wall. The water came from the *guaria* on the outside wall of our house, through a pipe that had been drilled through the bathroom wall and was situated over the cement tub. My Dad would fill the *guaria* each morning from the outside, and by night the sun would have heated the water to just about the right temperature for a nice warm shower.

Dad and I used to enjoy working on projects around the compound. One day during eighth-grade Christmas break, I found an old motorbike that one of the missionaries had left for jagga. Dad and I repaired it together, and I had a great time riding it all over the compound. Riding the motorbike gave me a sense of being free and reminded me of when Maria and I used to ride the horses together. It had been over two years since that night at the train station, but anything that reminded me of Maria was bittersweet. I still missed her so much.

The motorbike was functional as well as recreational because the compound was rather large. The other family who lived next door to us had a son, Tom, who also went to KA. He was three years younger than I. Tom's father was the overseer of the entire station. He was a very quiet man, but always had a smile on his face. He was a busy man, but never too busy to stop and say "hi" and give you a big hug. Tom's mother was a nurse and spent her days at the leprosarium. I used to watch her bandage the open sores of the lepers and wonder how she could keep from getting leprosy. She was so gentle, loving, and caring, and never seemed to mind the smell. They were a nice family, and we all liked them very much. We used to visit each other all the time just like neighbors did in America. We were quite lucky to be friends with a family that we liked so much.

Of all the leprosy work in the history of our mission, I heard of only one missionary who actually got leprosy. She lost all of her toes and walked with short steps, having to lean forward. I never realized how important toes were to our overall sense of balance. But according to the mission, she had never worked with lepers, and the disease was never life-threatening to her because she had it treated immediately. There may have been more missionaries who contracted the disease, but she was the only one of which I had ever heard.

The closest town to us was about twenty kilometers away, or about twelve and a half miles. The road that led to Minna, a city in West Central Nigeria, was right in front of our compound. Minna was the capital of Niger State, and Minna was where we purchased all of our supplies. Since it was Christmas of 1964, we were having a Christmas social gathering on the station. Our family had just arrived, and we didn't know many of the missionaries from the surrounding areas. Several of the missionaries from the outlying bush areas had come in to our station to celebrate Christmas with us.

A young, single, missionary lady in her late twenties and I had driven into Minna to get some supplies for our celebration. I was allowed to call her "Miss Carol" instead of "Auntie." I had met her in Kano while Mother and my Dad were in Language school, and we had become friends. We used to sit up in her little one-room cottage in Kano and eat fresh pineapple until our mouths would turn raw, and we would talk for hours. I asked her about being a teenager in the States, and we talked about music. Sometimes we even tried to find some rock music on the BBC of London radio station. I think she was a little lonely, too, and, of course, so was I.

It took us about forty-five minutes to get to Minna, travelling on rough, potted, dirt roads the whole way. Just as we pulled up in front of the little shop where we were headed for supplies, we heard a loud thud. I turned and saw an old beggar man. What happened seemed to be in slow motion as I watched his hip meet the front side of the car where I was sitting. His head, immediately following the impact, hit the windshield right before my eyes. The sound was sickening. The glass cracked, and the man slid down the front right side of the hood to the ground. It was like watching a horror movie, but as Miss Carol slammed on her breaks, and I slid forward towards the windshield with a jolt, the movie abruptly ended.

People gathered around our car talking excitedly. Different cultures have different norms about personal space. Even in a crowd, most Americans like at least six to twelve inches around them. On the other hand, most Africans forget any concept of personal space and prefer to get as close to the action as humanly possible, even if that means falling over one another and blocking each other's vision. That is exactly what began to happen. People out for their daily shopping, business people, anyone that happened to be walking by, just stopped and started pressing against our car and around the injured man.

Miss Carol turned off the engine of the car. "Stay in the car and don't look at anybody. Don't even move!" she hissed. I was terrified. I knew of another missionary woman who had just been placed in an African prison for running over a local Nigerian. He had crawled up under her car to escape the midday equatorial sun and it never occurred to her to look under the back of her car before she got in, backed up, and accidently ran over him. This was a time of great unrest in Nigeria, and it didn't take much to incite a riot of any kind. Especially when white people were involved, things were apt to become inflammatory.

"Dear Jesus, what should we do?" Miss Carol asked. Was she talking to me or to God? Was she as terrified as I was? But I knew even then that the prayer was more for herself than for the African that lay lifeless on the street. A crowd was growing, and they were beginning to bang their hands on the trunk. I knew we had to do something quickly. I just didn't know what. Miss Carol got out of the car and went around to check on the old man. She bent down and spoke to him in Hausa, trying to arouse him. She had to push her way through the crowd. I stayed in the car as told, not looking at anyone. A few minutes later, Miss Carol opened the back door and with help, lifted him into the back seat where he lay motionless. Then she then came around to the driver's seat and got in.

He opened his eyes to look around, and when I saw that he was alive, I was temporarily relieved. Then I realized she had put him in the car. I wanted to scream out, "Are you crazy?" There were no white people who could be used as witnesses or who could help us, just the growing crowds of local spectators.

"What are you doing?" I asked, trembling. "Where are you taking him?" The crowd was pressing against the car, trying to see inside.

"Be quiet," she said sternly. "I'm trying to think." I sure understood that. Thinking was hard to do amid the chaos and panic. Miss Carol blew the horn to clear the crowd and slowly pulled out into the road. She kept looking out of the rearview mirror to see if anyone was following us. I was especially hoping that the police had not been alerted as that would have really complicated things, and we might have very well ended up in an African jail with no help. We rode in silence for about ten minutes—the only sound the awful moaning of *baba*. I was so worried about him.

Finally, Miss Carol turned to me and said, "We are taking him to the government hospital." My heart stopped a moment. I had heard stories about most of the government hospitals. They were poorly staffed and very often resources were inadequate. Patients had been known to be left unattended for days if they were there alone.

Surprised, I asked, "Why aren't you taking him to our mission hospital?" She started fidgeting and did not answer my question. It occurred to me that perhaps she wanted to keep this whole accident as quiet as possible. The government hospital was quite a distance away, and we were already running late to get back to the mission party. Because of the accident, we hadn't even gotten a chance to buy our supplies. Miss Carol pulled up to the front of the main entrance, where a crowd sat on the front veranda. She told me to keep my head down low and stay in the car.

"Under no circumstances do you get out of this car!" she said.

"I promise I won't." She didn't have to worry, because I was afraid of what could happen to us. I was hoping the man would be alright, but I was also hoping that no one would find out who had hurt him. Miss Carol called to one of the Nigerians waiting at the front of the hospital to help her carry the hurt man from the car to the waiting area. They lay the man down on the floor close to the front door. Miss Carol jogged back to the car, got in, and we drove away. I'll never know how long it was before he got help, or the extent of his injuries. We were both sure they weren't life threatening, though, because of the heaviness and angle of the impact. The guilt has stayed with me even though there was nothing I could have done.

"Where are we going?" I asked.

"Home," she said curtly.

After that, neither of us ever mentioned the incident. She never told me not to tell my parents or anyone else, but from the way she had handled the situation, I just knew it should never be mentioned again. When we arrived back at the compound, after dark, everyone was concerned about us. We had "run out of gas," Miss Carol told everyone, and they were glad we were safe. Miss Carol avoided eye contact with me. I felt guilty about lying and feared someone could have recognized us as missionaries and reported us to the officials.

As the days dragged on, I was sure we would be reported to the police or mission, but we didn't hear anything. No government vehicles drove up. No soldiers with rifles threatening to take us off to a Nigerian jail. No word from the mission. So I began to relax a little. I still worried about the man who had been hurt. I still felt guilt and shame about the lies. I thought about Miss Carol. She, being the adult, assumed more of the responsibility of what happened. It was much harder on her. I missed Miss Carol and her friendship. She left to go back to her station, and I only saw her one other time. We never got a chance to speak, to share our feelings about the accident. I always thought that hitting the man and the events that followed put too much of a strain on our relationship. It would have helped me to have her to talk through my feelings about the accident. I think it would have helped her as well. But it didn't work out that way. Secrets have a way of ruining friendships.

Life wasn't always so dramatic when we were living in Chanchaga, but it always kept us on our toes. When you live in the bush, you can't just run to the doctor every time you get a chest cold or a boil on your leg. Many times you have to take matters into your own hands. Boils were as common in Africa as colds were in America in winter. That summer in Chanchaga, I had a boil, a huge boil, on the bend of my knee. It hurt so bad that I was writhing on the floor in pain. Boils can be excruciating until the pus head or core is removed. The pain had been building up for days. Finally, Mother called in the compound nurse and she told us that the core would have to come out to relieve the pressure.

Mother, and the nurse tried their best all afternoon to rid me of my affliction. They soaked it with hot cloths. No results. They put a poultice of sugar, bread, and sweet milk on it. That didn't work. It's an old remedy, but it usually works. Finally, the nurse looked at my boil very closely for several minutes. She promptly got up, left the room with Mother, and returned with a jar of petroleum jelly. She put about a half teaspoon fully covering the head of the boil. After a minute or so, it started to move. Slowly and quite painfully, a maggot emerged from the center of that Vaseline. Though that may sound gross to some, my pain was so relieved I could have kissed that little bugger. I was beaming.

I would have the pleasure of performing the same procedure on Ann the following year and having another one taken out of my other leg a year later. These parasites would even get on our little Dachshund. They were nasty, but a part of tropical life. A certain type of fly lays their eggs on your skin, and the larvae burrow into your skin and grow.

My poor brother, Edward, was plagued with the real kind of boils. He would continually get them on his fingers around his nail areas and he would spend countless hours soaking the affected finger in hot, salty water. I would go sit with him in the KA Infirmary and try to get his mind off of soaking his boils because this was a painful process. The heat from the hot water would draw out the pus. And when the boil was tight, the pus would actually shoot out with the pressure of his heartbeat. He couldn't help but cry from the pain. But when the pressure was released, it felt so much better. When we first arrived in Africa, he didn't know what was happening to him, he got them so often. Boils and maggots emerging from your skin didn't happen much in the States! It was all a part of culture shock.

Towards the end of summer, I started packing my clothes, getting ready to go back to school for ninth grade. I wasn't in the best of moods. Unexpectedly, my Dad and I were invited by another missionary, named Uncle Will, to visit a village about an hour outside of Chanchaga. He was originally from Britain, and he lived at a neighboring mission station. Anytime I got a chance to go bush with my Dad, I took it, as it was always exciting.

The three of us left a few days later. We started out early in the morning, and at eight o'clock it was already eighty degrees. Dad told me to be on time as Uncle Will was going to collect us, and he was a stickler for time. We got there a couple of minutes early.

"Ah, spot on!" said Uncle Will in approval, pulling out his pocket watch to check the time, his jeep sputtering and hissing close by. We set out on a typically rough and bumpy dirt road. During the first half hour, we didn't pass any other villages, and we hardly passed any people. I could tell we were headed towards a very isolated area. Nobody talked much during the car ride. Uncle Will was very different from Mr. Peterson, the man who had taken us to see the Fulani Beatings. Mr. Peterson was jovial, talkative, and friendly. Uncle Will was on the quiet side and seemed to me rather stern, but I was thankful to him for taking us on this adventure.

Soon, the road ended, and we got out and walked along a wide pathway. It began to narrow. We were far into the bush, which was full of small game. The bush provided the villagers with meat and held lots of vegetation. As far as the eye could see, the landscape was scattered with beautiful acacia trees and thick underbrush difficult to walk through. But the walking paths were well worn and direct. After following the path for about twenty-five minutes, we came to a clearing. Out of nowhere, several children came running up to us. As soon as they saw me, they backed up and started talking excitedly among themselves. They ran back into the village. I asked Uncle Will why they were acting as if they were frightened of me. He said he wasn't sure if a young white girl had ever been to this village, and the children may be looking at one for the first time.

At first I was intimidated, but once we were in the village, the children became a little surer of themselves because their parents were nearby. Soon, I drew a crowd. When I walked in Africa, I always tried to take some candy with me, hoping to see some children. Children who live in the bush don't often get candy, and they are so grateful for it. Children of all shapes and sizes wanted to see what I was giving out. It helped them overcome their fear of me. Closer and closer they came, their little hands beginning to touch mine. They pulled on my dress, and the braver ones were fascinated by my long, straight blond hair. They would run it through their fingers and giggle with delight, and I would rub my hand over their heads as well. One of the ladies of the village brought me a zane (rhymes with Connie), a wrap-around cloth which can be worn alone or over another dress piece, and showed me how to wear it. I wore it for the duration of our visit. It was such a kind gesture and made me feel so at home.

A loud burst of laughter from the adult group disrupted my play with the children. I joined the group which included my Dad, Uncle Will, the Chief, and a few other men from the village.

Uncle Will began to translate the conversation they were having. "Well, Miss Cheryl, the Chief here has just made a very generous offer for your hand in marriage."

Startled, I looked at my Dad and said, "Oh, but I am too young!"

"Oh, he doesn't mind your age," Dad replied, "but he does think you need to be fattened up a little."

I knew African girls married at puberty, and I was pretty skinny, but surely Dad was pulling another one of his tricks. Before I was really convinced of that and knew what was happening, my Dad said, "Oh, there's one other problem... the chief didn't offer enough. For you he offered one goat, two pigs, and four chickens. If he would have offered one more goat, he would have had a deal."

For a moment, I was confused. By then, I thought Dad was kidding, and yet I did not want to offend anyone for their hospitality. At the same time, I did not fully understand the look in the chief's eyes as all of this was taking place. My Dad said later that the chief was serious, but of course Dad was kidding, although I did not know this for sure until we were back in the jeep. Dad would tease me about that for many years to come. "One more goat and you would have been an African Queen!" he used to say.

Thankfully, the children had tired of waiting for me to come back and had come over to steal me away from the adult group. We started back with our childish play, much to my relief. But my African fantasies often led me to think what my life would have been like as an African sister or wife and mother. I had taken in that much of Africa at only fourteen. I was that comfortable in this country.

Chapter Ten

Parents Living at Kent Academy

From left to right: My little sister, Ann, holding our dog Prince; then me, next to me is my mother; then my Dad, and tucked under my Dad's arm is my brother Edward.

In January of 1965, I flew, along with my parents, brother and sister, and of course, Prince, in the Piper Aztec to Jos. We were then living in Chanchaga, so the flight was not uncomfortably long. The six of us had the plane to ourselves. One of the KA uncles picked us up in a van and took us to KA.

This time, instead of studying the sites and people along the ride which is what I usually like to do, first I thought about the future. These were the last few months of my fourth year at KA. My parents were going to be house parents there for six months, from January to June. In June, we would return to the US for furlough. If or when I returned, I would be going to Hillcrest High School, and the twins would return to KA. My parents would be re-stationed again to another new town or village, another new house, a place as yet undetermined. I didn't understand my feelings about all of these coming changes; but I had faced a lot worse over the past several years, and change had become the only constant in my life.

In six short months, I would be back in Georgia with my sister, Maria. With all that my family and I had gone through in the last three and a half years, I felt guilty at times for almost forgetting about her. We were so close and when I first came to Africa, I thought of her every day. But as time would have it, my thoughts got busy with boarding school, friends, and avoiding unpleasant aunties and uncles. I would go a few days without thinking about her, but she was never far from my heart. With my family here, I could endure anything for six months. I thought I was the happiest I had been in a long time.

Mother had bought all of us new outfits from the Sears and Roebuck catalogue for Christmas so we wouldn't look like we had just crawled out of a missionary barrel when we arrived in the States. I was grateful for that, even though the dress was a little outdated—at least by my limited knowledge of US fashions and from what I saw in *Time Magazine*. Our reading material was heavily censored: no teen magazines, or other racy magazines, no *Gone with the Wind,* no *Catcher in the Rye,* and others.

We arrived a few days before the rest of the students so we could move into our house. The twins and I were given a choice. We could either live in the dorm with the kids, or we could live in the house with our parents. Well, for goodness sake! Which would you choose? We chose to live in the house with our parents. It was a relatively nice place. The front door opened up into the center of the playground with the view of a huge beautiful mango (yuk!) tree about twenty-five to thirty feet high. The back door opened into the lobby of the little girls' dormitory.

I knew the moment I entered the house that my parents were no longer going to be my own. They now belonged to every student who attended school at KA. The kids could stop them anytime to ask them a question, they could hug them anytime they wanted to, and could come up to our door and knock on it for any reason at any time day or night. I realized this was what I would have to get used to because that was their job as dorm parents. I never got completely comfortable with this feeling. But to be with my parents, I had to share my parents.

The first month went by smoothly. My Dad worked on a few new things at KA that the kids thought were terrific, like the rabbit hutches. He grew rabbits to supplement the food supply for the school, and he recruited the older boys to go down and help him take care of the animals. They built the pens, and Dad designed a watering system for them. The design was simple, yet effective. The rabbit pens were built side by side in rows. Right through the front of each cage, a long, continuous water pipe was secured. With a small cut-out in the pipe in front of each cage, the rabbits had access to fresh, clean flowing water from which they could drink.

Dad also helped the boys build soap box cars. The boys would hold soap box car races on Saturday. The girls loved to watch and cheer. He allowed the kids to eat the fruit from the fruit trees located down by the chapel in front of the cemetery if it was on the ground. None of the other aunties or uncles that I knew of would allow the kids to eat fruit at all. So after a hard African rain, when all the lemons, oranges, grapefruits, mangoes, and guavas got knocked off the trees, all the kids knew Uncle Rolan would let you eat the fruit that had been beaten to the ground. I think this ultimately got him in trouble with the other staff, but he told me there was no reason that good fruit on the ground should go to waste, and it was a dumb rule to let it rot!

Mother also established a habit of her own. She personally tried to tuck as many young girls as she could into bed when she was on night duty. She didn't even do that to me and the twins at home every night. I was surprised, but I was secretly glad she did that, because I knew some of those kids were just as confused and lonely as I was. All they needed was lots of love and care, and they needed as much as they could get.

Those last six months of ninth grade were the happiest since I'd left my home. Edward, Ann, and I were living together with our parents. That's all we really wanted. We were all getting along, and it was time to start packing our things to come back to the States on furlough. We were excited. During that time, I had changed from a skinny kid into a young lady, and Edward and Ann had grown from toddlers to elementary students. I was afraid that Maria wouldn't even know us. And would we know her?

Mother and my Dad were probably more anxious about seeing Maria than I. Maria, almost nineteen, had gotten married a few months ago to a young man they didn't know. They couldn't understand why she didn't wait until they came home so they could meet him and be at her wedding. I guess I could understand their point of view, but we all knew Maria had a terrible time while we were away in Africa. She had gone from living with the family at the church, to living with my grandmother, to my aunt and uncle on Mother's side, to my aunt and uncle on my Dad's side, and finally back to grandmother's house. None of those living arrangements were easy on her. She lost her real home the night we left her at the train station. I think part of the reason she got married was to have a place of her own where she could be safe. I was completely in favor of her going ahead and getting married, even if it meant I, or our family, couldn't be at her wedding. If she was happy, I was happy. I had often felt some guilt for my sister because she had given up so much when she was left behind. She probably thought we were all out in Africa on this great, exciting adventure. I never told her my side of the story. She knew nothing of my loneliness, the pain, and the numbness. Our letters were always censored. But that was behind us now, and we were on our way home.

And June finally, finally rolled around after what seemed like an eternity of studying and exams. I passed, graduating from ninth grade in a class of about twenty other MKs. Some were going to the States to attend Christian boarding schools for the rest of their high school years, some were going straight on to Hillcrest High in Jos, and some were going on furlough, like me. It was often hard to make and keep friends in Africa as all of them were continually scattered. I never knew who would be leaving when or if they would ever come back, so as a result I found it hard to trust people. You got close to people, and they would leave. *No Coke, Only Fanta, right?*

For my entire ninth grade at school, all I could think about was going back home to the States, being a real teenager, and going to a real high school. It was what we MKs referred to as "being normal kids." Every semester or so, one or two kids would come back from the States with the latest fashion, haircut, and pictures. They would tell us what it was like to be in the States again. We would all sit around and listen with excitement, eager for our turn, and missing what we remembered of our homeland, friends, and family so far away. My day came on June 18, 1965.

We were packed and ready to go back to the US, to my cousins, my grandparents, to a few friends that I remembered back home. I wondered what it would feel like. We didn't own a house. Africa felt more like my home now. Torn between two places, I felt like a lost child.

Chapter Eleven
American Culture Shock

My family and I flew out of Kano, Nigeria, and over to Europe for a few days of sight-seeing. I wanted to fly straight home, but my parents thought that we should take advantage of the opportunities to see England and Scotland. That would make three countries in Europe that I had seen so far. I had to admit, I was becoming somewhat of a real travel bug. I had begun collecting souvenirs and postcards, and Mother made us all wait on her at each location until she had picked out the perfect collector's spoon for her new collection.

We were traveling with some other missionaries who were close friends of my parents. We all got along well and planned the trip together. We toured all of the famous sights in London, including the changing of the guards. We saw the famous castles in Scotland. My greatest memory of the trip home, though, was how happy everyone was, especially Mother and Dad. Our whole family was always laughing and smiling in spite of the long, tiring trip. At first, it seemed strange spending so much time together with Mother and Dad, almost a sense of normalcy. Even with them living at the school, we rarely ate with them or spent much time with them except at night when we went to bed, or on their days off. So on the trip, we were all thrown together, and it was like getting to know them all over again, but under the best of circumstances.

After four days of travel, we arrived in New York, the same mission headquarters where we first started out four years ago, 164 West 74th Street. And then things changed. Mother and Dad became very serious, almost worried, all the time. Mother made us stay very quiet any time we were out of our room. "Children are to be seen and not heard," she would say.

My Dad would be in New York long enough for us to get our mandatory medical check-ups by the mission doctor and for Mother and my Dad to do the necessary paper work for returning missionaries. I guess they had already decided to go back for another four-year term, although it had not been discussed with us, the children. That meant I would spend the rest of my high school years in Africa and graduate at Hillcrest. This was the very high school I found out Mother and my Dad could have sent my sister four years earlier to but didn't because of theological arguments SIM was having with another member mission. I often thought what a difference it could have made in my sister's life, in our family's lives, had she been able to come to Africa with us.

Maria and her new husband, Allen, had driven their car from Atlanta to meet us. They would drive my family and me back down to Atlanta. They arrived on the day as planned, and we were packed and ready to go. Our dog, Prince, was to be flown directly to Atlanta and would arrive soon after we arrived.

When I first saw Maria get out of her car on that busy New York street in front of the mission, I thought she looked like a beautiful young woman. She was just under twenty years old with a modern hairstyle and sophisticated clothing. No longer did I see the tomboy I had admired all my life, who taught me everything I knew about horses and how to care for them, and who slung cut bales of hay off a truck. She was a young lady now and married at that. I felt proud of her but angry that I had missed four years of her life. The twins hugged her and laughed with joy. They didn't seem to notice the differences the years had made, but their laughs and hugs broke the tension, as they always did. Maria turned to me.

"You've grown, girl," she said. Yep, that was still my sister. She always called me "girl." I guess I needed to be reassured. Life can be so unreal at times. It plays tricks on you, some of them cruel. I wanted to tell her everything then, as we stood there. I wanted to tell her about how sorry I was we left her even though I didn't have a choice. I wanted to tell her about my pain and wanted to know about hers. I even wanted to tell her about what the faceless monster doctor did and my episodes of "going away." Instead, I gazed over at Maria's new husband and back at her. I saw the way she looked at him and hoped she now had someone who could take care of her and love her. I wondered if it would ever be the same between us. I wanted it to be, but I knew we had both lost our innocence and somehow it was going to be different because we were both different. Maria would be sleeping down the hall that night with a strange man in the mission home. We got to know Allen a little that night at dinner, but he was shy and still more of a stranger to us. He was my parents' son-in-law, suddenly thrust in, and my brother-in-law, as well. We all realized it, but none of us said it— "It is not the same." My sister was also a stranger to us. Even their southern accents seemed foreign, and we did not realize that over the years in Africa we had lost most of ours. People here in the States told us that we had more of a British-sounding accent.

That night, I crawled into an American bed for the first time in four years. Yes, beds have their own characteristics from country to country. These beds were like the old antique, dark metal beds that my grandmother used to have in her house. Spring beds with one mattress that was about four or five inches thick, but comfortable enough. Still, the happenings of the day were too much for me, and I quietly "went away." My body stiffened, my jaws clenched, my eyes shut tight, and my breathing slowed. The deep, black hole appeared, and I willingly fell into it, forever falling. The numbness was my temporary refuge.

We met for breakfast in the dining hall the next morning. The director rang the little bell to call everyone to be seated. Thirty or thirty-five people sat at the breakfast tables. When everyone was seated and quiet, the director began the same morning routine that was carried out across most mission stations sharing breakfast.

"Our morning devotional is taken from Romans 6:23 KJV: 'For the wages of sin is death, but the gift of God is eternal life through Jesus Christ our Lord.'" And then he would talk about the verse (stomach growls) for a few minutes and how it could (more stomach growls) help us through our day. He would end in

137

a prayer and (more growls along with a few heavy sighs) a blessing for our food. It was a miracle I made it through devotions each morning. But I did, and on this occasion, we headed straight for the car.

On the way back to Georgia, it was crowded in the car, but we managed. My parents, Maria, Allen, the twins, and I were just happy to be back together. It was all so surreal being back in the States.

We made one stop before leaving New York City. The 1964/1965 New York World's Fair was going on in Queens. World's Fairs are special events, and Maria and Allen and my parents were excited about it. So we spent a day at the fair. My favorite rides were the monorail and the Log Flume. I also enjoyed some of the exhibits, like GE's Home of the Future. But the timing wasn't great. I was experiencing a little culture shock at the fair. The huge crowds of white people seemed so strange to me. The amounts of food everywhere, its abundance, and how much was wasted and thrown away shocked me. People were loud and boisterous. The women and girls were dressed so immodestly. Maybe it was just the environment of the park, but I was uncomfortable. I found myself missing the greens and the breezes, the peace and gentleness of Africa, instead of this concrete world. Everybody was in a hurry. People didn't greet you like they did in Africa, taking the time to acknowledge you and your family. The clothing, the beehive hairstyles, all seemed like something out of a comic book. By the end of the day, I was exhausted and feeling homesick, but not really sure where home was.

The rest of our trip to Georgia was uneventful and was given over to getting to know each other again while either cooped up in the car or in the motel room. We all stayed clear of heavy conversations. Nothing but pleasantries. I thought that strange. We did get to know Allen better as he shared some information about his childhood and his family. When he started, he was a real talker which helped the time go by.

We didn't talk much about the wedding. I know my parents wanted Maria and Allen to wait until they came home for furlough so they could see them get married and meet Allen before the ceremony. But Allen came along and Maria fell in love with him. He was educated and seemingly financially secure and could offer her a home that she needed. They became engaged. At the time, she was a young eighteen-year-old. My parents had the choice to come home for the wedding, or to talk her out of it, or to give her a home and the love that she desperately needed. They chose to stay on the field, putting God's work before their daughter.

We talked a bit about our relatives, how everyone was doing, and how exciting it was going to be to see everybody. We talked about everything except what was really on our minds. Mother, my Dad, and I wanted to know about what had happened to my sister while we were gone. And didn't she want to know about my school? How we had lived? But nothing really important was ever talked about. We were pent up in that car for three and a half days driving from New York City to Stone Mountain, Georgia, and nothing meaningful was ever mentioned. No one spoke of the elephant in the car. That's the way it was in my family. No one talked about difficult issues.

When we arrived in Georgia, the church that supported Mother and Dad's mission work had rented a house for us to live. It was a little frame house in a low-rent neighborhood, decorated by Goodwill, but the rent was paid for us until my Dad found work. I felt embarrassed. Our houses in Africa looked nicer than this one. Mother took a look at my forlorn face and said that we should be grateful. Yes, I *should* be grateful, but I also noticed the look of disappointment and embarrassment on her own face as well. Why did people think that just because we were missionaries we deserved less in everything? Did they think we enjoyed sacrifice?

It was September, and the days were starting to get cold. It was the first cold weather I had experienced in four years. I also started my tenth grade in a real American high school, Towers High School. It was exciting spending most of the summer preparing for the first day—what I would wear, how I would act, what would I say to the kids, etc. I had clothes to buy. I needed to learn the popular singers and how to do my hair in a new style. Yet, I was totally unprepared for what was to come.

Mother drove me the first day. As I got out of the car, I became one in a sea of over a thousand high school students. Boy, did I stick out in my brand new white tennis shoes and bobby socks, and homemade shift dress with cotton ball trim cut to Mother's requirement of three inches below the knee. Most all the other girls were wearing miniskirts. And, my hair looked a little strange as well. We didn't keep up with American hairstyles at Hillcrest. I was different, and those first few months were quite difficult. Kids can be cruel. Their looks, the snide comments, and the isolation of eating lunch by myself began to put pressures on me that I didn't know how to handle.

My "going away" and splitting became more common place. I was too shy to make friends. I didn't even know any of the kids at our church well enough to talk to them. I wore outdated, hand-me-down clothes. I didn't know anything about American culture, like politics, pop music, or references to movie stars. There had been no TV or radio for us to watch or listen to in Africa at KA. I had nothing in common with kids my age. I couldn't relate to American kids, and they couldn't relate to me. By habit, I was still jutting out my chin to point to things, the Nigerian way of pointing, instead of using my finger. I would accidentally use Hausa words in my everyday speech such as "*Kai*" (rhymes with "Hi"), like Americans might use "Wow," and they would look at me like I was crazy. The same way I had not been prepared for the differences in culture when I moved to Africa, I was also not prepared for reintegration back into the United States. The sixties were turbulent times in America and a lot had changed.

Not all of the culture shock was negative, though. When I left Georgia in 1960, there were no enclosed shopping malls. Mostly, there were shopping areas or plazas. When we returned in 1964, shopping malls were becoming quite popular, with "moving stairs" between floors and restaurants. I saw my first touch-tone phone, got my first halogen lamp, and oohed and aahed over Maria's audio cassette player.

Things began to change when I was introduced to pop music. I was allowed to spend the weekend with Maria, and she loved Leslie Gore. We listened to her music all weekend, and I was hooked. We danced and played in her den. There was something in the music that opened me up. It triggered a sense of awareness that the way I had been living and feeling about my life had not been right.

We played the music loud, and I felt my body moving to the words and vibrations. I found myself trying to memorize the words to the songs and I related to them in a strong way.

"You don't own me." Leslie sang out.

"Don't tell me what to do. Don't tell me what to say." I sang loudly along with Leslie. It felt freeing to sing out against all of the rules and restrictions of living an institutional life, even as hard as I had tried to fit in.

"And please, when I go out with you, don't put me on display."

Being a MK meant always being on display of some sort or another. We were expected to set an example for everyone as children of God, but as our parents were called as missionaries, we MKs had to adhere to an even higher standard than people in our school and our church. I resented my parents more than ever for constantly placing that pressure on me now that we were on furlough. This played out by my having to wear a split skirt on a church ice skating social. Mother didn't believe in Christian ladies wearing pants in public. Since this was my first time ice skating, I ending up showing more of myself than I would have if I had worn a pair of pants.

"Just let me be myself, that's all I ask of you," Leslie Gore and I sang on. As I got more and more into the words, I thought about my time at KA, and I realized that while I loved Africa and the people of Nigeria, I was becoming aware of an intense anger deep inside me from experiences at KA and my non-existent home life. This anger would continue to grow.

Maria gave me an old transistor radio, and I found some great rock stations. From then on, I began to listen carefully to the words and memorized the songs that had meaning to me. Since my parents and the mission as a whole were against rock and roll, I had to be careful not to let my parents know I was listening to such "bad and sinful" music. This made me feel even more guilty. All the kids at school and even the girls at church listened to music and their parents let them. Not mine. All the girls wore pants and even shorts. Not me. I had to be that perfect

MK, a Christian example all the time. This caused some pretty heated arguments with Mother. Our biggest argument was whether or not I could stay home from Sunday night church to see the Beatles on the Ed Sullivan TV show, just the biggest event of my life at the time. Well, I should have known not to even ask. But ask, I did.

It occurred to me through this experience, an epiphany, if you will, that all of my religious upbringing had been false or lacking. I realized that I had no real relationship with God. I had "asked Jesus to save me" when I was six. But there was no real understanding behind that event. From then on it was, "Don't do this, don't do that or God will punish you or you will go to hell." My Christianity was based on doing good deeds and guilt, not a relationship with a loving God. But by this point in my life, I really didn't think such a relationship possible. There was too much anger in me. I felt truly lost.

"Cheryl Elizabeth King, you ought to be ashamed of yourself," screamed Mother. She hovered over me as she continued, "First of all, to ask not to go to church is sinful enough, but to ask for such a reason. To hear a rock and roll band of devil singers instead of being in God's house is unforgiveable. Go to your room and ask for the Lord's forgiveness. You are also grounded, young lady. We will talk more about it tomorrow."

"But, Mother, some of the kids from the church are staying home to watch it together." This was the truth, but I should have known better than to say it to Mother.

She raised her hand to slap me across the face, but I ducked and stepped back. As I got older, I had learned how to avoid a few of those slaps. The key was being quick. She didn't pursue me this time and simply said, "I don't care what anyone at the church does, you are not doing it!" And of course, I didn't, or it would be a hard slap on the face or a belting. My parents believed in corporal punishment although Dad left it mostly up to Mother to implement. I can remember only once my Dad laying a hand on me.

One of the hardest things for me to get used to the year we were home on furlough was going with my parents to different churches to do deputation work. I understood the importance of staying in touch with all of the people who had supported us financially the last four years, and also that we needed additional support for the next four years, since we were going back to Africa. It was the method that was difficult for me.

We would visit a church that had or would support us for a four-year term, which was the common agreement, usually on a Sunday morning. My parents would meet and greet their friends and new members of the church while we, the kids, stood quietly by in case questions were asked of us. When the service began, our family would sit in the front of the church, and my Dad would speak if not preach the sermon. Then he would tell the congregation about their work on the mission field and about his children's lives at boarding school (or at least what he knew). Mother would try to get me to say a few words about school, but I always refused because I was so shy, and because I didn't want to lie in church. It made me physically sick to my stomach to even think about getting up and speaking to a congregation about KA. Dad would always tell them about our need for their continued prayers and for their financial support as well as other needs that might have been pressing at the time.

The pastor might lead the benediction while our family would be taken to the front of the church to face the congregation so that the members could walk down the line and shake hands with each one of us. Some people would slip money into my Dad's hand. A few people refused to shake our hands because we had lived and worked at a leprosarium. One time a lady put some money in my hand and said, "You can use this to get your mommy to buy you a new dress." I was mortified. That is certainly not something a fourteen-year-old wants to hear, but a quick look down at the hand-me-down dress I was wearing made me realize she was right. I could use a nicer dress.

This was also when people would hug us, shake hands with us, and tell us what wonderful Christian people we were. I guess they meant well, but their words never rang true to me. Yes, missionaries were supposed to be good Christian people, but not all of them were. In fact, over the past four years of my life in Africa, I found too many of them that weren't good people at all, after my experiences. Why was this the case? Why had this been my experience? I was searching for answers and, finding none, it was still easy to blame myself. There must be something inherently bad within me. If I were good, bad things would not happen to me. God would have protected me as He promised, wouldn't He?

The school year was just about over, and our furlough time was coming to an end. I had gotten over enough of my shyness to make some friends. Although I missed Africa, I had just begun to feel comfortable in America again. And so I began talking to Mother and Dad about letting me stay home with Maria and her husband, Allen, for my last two years of high school. While I thought it was a great idea, my parents were vehemently opposed. There was no consideration of the idea. So I tried another avenue, one I knew Mother would seriously consider.

"What if Hillcrest High doesn't offer the courses that I need to get into nursing school? Then can I stay?" I asked desperately, knowing that Mother's big wish was for me to go to Georgia Baptist Nursing School.

At Mother's urging, I was destined to become a missionary nurse. But after my sophomore year in a public school, I began to realize just how many interesting careers there were in the world. And, 1965 was the beginning of the women's movement— equality and liberation for all women. I could become a doctor instead of a nurse, or anything else I could dream of. I just hadn't started dreaming yet. But the mission was not big on career options in parochial schools unless it was one related to the clergy, at least in the very strict, fundamental one in which I lived. At any rate, my parent's considered the question and after contacting Hillcrest in Jos, Nigeria, we found out that they did not offer Latin, a course that was required for entry into the nursing school to which I had already applied, Georgia Baptist Hospital School of Nursing. Unfortunately for me, they found out just in time I could take it at Hillcrest through a correspondence course. So that was that. I was to learn Latin through correspondence. I was on my way back to Africa. Things could be worse. I could have been going back to KA.

The last month was spent packing for my last two years of high school. I would then be flying back to New York alone upon graduating from Hillcrest High. I realized that at this time I would leave my entire family to live in yet another dormitory for three years of nursing school in Atlanta, Georgia, and not see them again until I was approaching twenty. When my parents became missionaries and left Maria that night at the train station when I was ten years old, little did I realize that would be the last real sense of a home with my parents, the twins, and Maria I would ever have again.

My parents, Edward, and Ann had to pack for another four years. Since we had left all of our belongings in Africa, we needed only to focus on clothes and other things of convenience that may help in daily life. I bought as many store-bought clothes as I could: bell bottoms, ruffled blouses, hip huggers. I made a few dresses with the new psychedelic fabric. I got Maria to take me shopping, and I bought some single records to take back: The Rolling Stones, The Beatles, The Animals, and, of course, Leslie Gore. But funds were scarce, and shopping trips few.

Between packing, we spent the last few weeks of furlough visiting friends and family. We stayed with my grandparents. I would never see Papa King again, my Dad's father. He died just weeks before we left. I so enjoyed getting to know him again during the past year. Such a gentle giant. When I was little, he loved to take me to the counter at the Old Stone Mountain Pharmacy, and buy me a lime sherbert cone, two scoops. Thanks, Papa King.

The big day soon arrived. We took a propjet back to New York for a short stay in the big city, just long enough for our shots, medical exams, and a few update meetings that my parents attended in the mission. The last week of July, 1966, we left for Nigeria.

On this trip we spent a few days in Switzerland. The beauty of the land and the snowy mountains were breathtaking. I had never seen such beauty. Mother got her souvenir spoon, and I got a small glass figurine to go with my giraffe. This time, I felt we didn't seem as jovial as on the way back to the States. My parents and the twins seemed reserved and preoccupied. Maybe it was just me. On July 29, 1966, we arrived in Kano, Nigeria, and spent a day or two at the Kano mission to get over jet lag. Then we were sent on to Ilorin which was to be my parents' new assignment and our next house.

Our beautiful home in Ilorin–made from stones and cement.

The front yard full of beautiful palm trees.

Like an Ancient Root

Like an ancient root,
dormant no longer
she climbed, twisted and
pushed her way
up out of the darkness
into the warmth.
All that stood in her way
was overwhelmed
by the passion of her intention
to bathe again
in the light.

— Anonymous

Chapter Twelve

So Scandalous

Our station in Ilorin was quite lovely. The grounds were well-manicured with palm trees blowing in the breeze, flowers planted all around, and white-washed rocks lining the drive. The house itself was completely made of stone. There was a round-about at the end of the drive next to our house so people could access a small building housing the Business Department (BD), and the guest houses, four small, one-bedroom, one-bath cottages that sat across from the drive.

Located in the western part of Nigeria, Ilorin is one of the larger cities. SIM has several bush stations in the surrounding areas, so the Ilorin station serves as a supply station for the missionaries at these outlying locations. It also has a mission airport. Dad's duties as Station Manager included running the BD which was like a small grocery store where the missionaries could stock up on food and supplies. I used to help

My parents inside the Business Department (BD), a mini grocery store with other supplies for the missionaries in the surrounding remote areas.

my Dad keep it stocked and clean. He also kept records for the station and did just about anything else that needed doing around the station.

Mother's duties were to keep the four little one-room guest houses clean and ready for any missionaries who showed up for supplies. She also ran the big stone house we lived in and prepared any and all meals which we ate together along with any missionary guests.

One of the great things about Ilorin was the European club right down the street from our house. It was a private membership club, and although missionaries were not allowed to join, club ownership would allow certain individuals to use the

Edward, my younger brother,
at the "club" in Ilorin.

facilities, such as the pool, for a small fee. I used to ride my bike to the club every day when I finished my chores. I would order chips, as the Brits called French fries, and use vinegar on them instead of ketchup in the British way. It's "jolly good" when you get used to it. Most times I would drink a Fanta. No Coke, Only Fanta! Although by 1966, Coke was getting easier to find in Nigeria! It was drinking Coke warm that was the problem for me. When you asked for ice, as only Americans did, you only got one, at most two pieces. The African sun was so hot that ice really didn't matter after two to three minutes anyway. It was great to sit by the pool eating chips and listening to the rock music they played over the speakers, sipping my warm Fanta or Coke.

"Et maintenant, le noir est noir!" the BBC radio announcer would blare out. "And now, Black is Black." It was one of my favorite songs, and I'd always sing along. "I want my baby back."

Unfortunately, the opportunity for me to get to know my new home was short lived, as I had to leave to go to my new school, Hillcrest High, only two weeks after we arrived back in

Africa. So once again, I was on one of our mission planes to Jos. By this time, traveling, leaving, and goodbyes, were all second nature to me. Did I still get lonely? Yes. But it wasn't for my parents like it used to be. It felt more like a piece of me was being torn away, like I was losing a little bit of myself. Split was a better way to describe it. I would just split and become my school self. I was sad a great deal after I first came back to Africa. I told myself the feeling would go away because I loved Africa. I couldn't understand why I was feeling depressed. But it didn't go away. Depression became my constant companion. But I told no one. Since any illness, according to Mother, was God's way of teaching us something, I wasn't going to appear weak. To hide the depression, I relied heavily on my wit and humor. Everything became a joke, and I tried to laugh everything off. Ironically, in my senior year, I was voted "wittiest in class." This was yet another one of my selves, my clown, or funny self. I could deflect the pain in my life by being funny.

The trip to Jos was a relatively short flight, only a couple of hours, and when I arrived, at least I didn't have the forty-five-minute drive to KA. Niger Creek Hostel, the home for the mission's high school students once they left KA, housed approximately twenty-five students. There was a living and dining area in between the girls' and boys' wings. My room was at the end of the girls' hall. I liked

The hostel where I lived for grades eleven and twelve.

that. It gave me the privacy for which I longed. I had a great roommate, Sarah, and it seemed that my junior year was off to a great start. The hostel was one of about ten other houses on the compound, and it was a fifteen-minute walk from the high school itself.

Hillcrest school was founded in July, 1942, for European and American children, but quickly expanded and grew to

Not
in
1966,
68!

include grades one through twelve and virtually any nationality. As a truly international school, and one very well-known across Nigeria, it was well attended by Africans, Asians, Middle Easterners, and missionary kids of differing denominations. Each day vans from different religious hostels drove into the Hillcrest parking area. There were thirty kids in my junior year class. Most of the hostels were represented in my class, and it made for interesting discussions. The environment was so much more open at Hillcrest than at KA.

Mr. and Mrs. Robbins, or Uncle Henry and Aunt Pat, were the house parents of the hostel. They had two young sons who went to KA during the week and stayed at the hostel in their private quarters on the weekends and holidays. They also had an older daughter who had graduated from high school and was living with them for the year. Uncle Henry was a big man who walked with a slight shuffle. I never felt he was comfortable in his role as house parent to a bunch of pimply faced teenagers. He would try to be your friend, but once he realized he was being nice, he would get serious and make sure he was enforcing all of the rules. Uncle Henry had a serious temper as well. I could never trust his reactions. Aunt Pat was a quiet, stern woman who went about trying to make a home for us. She kept us well fed and the hostel clean, but she wasn't a warm person. And I was never of the opinion that she liked her job. But we were all thrown together in this home-like environment and had this unrealistic expectation to live like a family.

We did have a little more freedom than we did at KA. Our letters home were not read. We could go into town, Jos, with Uncle Henry on the weekends to shop if we needed something. We could play our records quietly in our rooms if they had been approved. If there was a song Uncle Henry didn't approve of, he would scratch that song or those songs off the album with a pin. Of course, that would make the needle jump when it hit the forbidden song and then it would skip across the album, essentially ruining it. He scratched a song off my album, *Whipped Cream and Other Delights,* by Tijuana Brass. The song was "Love Potion #9." He said it was a strip tease song and was suggestive. He took gift wrapping paper and covered half of the cover of the album. He said the girl on the cover eating cake and icing would make the boys lust. I didn't dare show him my singles from the Animals and the Rolling Stones. I didn't want to take a chance on him objecting to the words and the beat of the songs. Rarely were we left alone at the hostel, but when we were, I'd run and get the Tijuana album and play it as loud as I dared, along with my singles.

My first year at Hillcrest was eleventh grade. I settled pretty well into school. I was under a lot of pressure for both my junior and senior year to make at least a B average if I expected to get into nursing school. I was not the best student around, more of a B- or C+ student. But when I really put forth all of my effort, I could usually maintain a B average. We had study hall in our dining room at the hostel every night from seven to nine o'clock, and that forced me to sit down and study. I got into a rhythm. I made new friends. I knew quite a few of the kids from KA. Being away from them in my sophomore year, it was strange to see how they had all grown up.

The day after I moved into the hostel, I found out that Renee, one of my friends from KA, and her family, lived next door to the hostel. Our friendship grew even stronger over our two years in high school. Renee had already been at Hillcrest a year and knew a lot of the kids. She introduced me to several of them. She also knew a lot of the British people in town, and I got to know some of them as well. Renee's father was from Great Britain and had a strong British accent. Her mother was from Maryland, and she used to make the best cinnamon rolls I had ever tasted. She used to make them on the weekends and would save one for me occasionally.

Renee and I spent a lot of time together, and even though she was a year younger than I, I looked up to her in many ways. She had an air of sophistication that I admired, and I was in awe of her self-confidence. I used to hang out at her house after school until the dinner bell. She showed me how to make, purchase, and apply make-up. It was difficult to find mascara in the local shops, so she showed me how to take the empty mascara container and mix black shoe polish with Vaseline. The trick was trying to get it back into the empty container again; but it worked just fine long as it didn't get in your eyes. It tended to smear quite easily and when it did, it burned! I didn't wear it very often because, by the end of the day, I tended to look like a raccoon.

Renee and I used to go into town together and hang out with friends or shop. The hostel kids weren't supposed to be in town without an adult, but Renee's Mom and Dad thought we were old enough and let us go with the promise to be safe. I loved those times being out on our own together. Sometimes Renee's boyfriend would meet us at the club in town. The club was much larger than the one in Ilorin, with a larger restaurant and pool. On the weekends, there were a lot of government people, expats, and we could catch up on a few new styles. But we also had to be careful not to be seen from anyone in the mission. Luckily, the missionaries usually didn't go to places in town that served drinks or held dances. They wanted to set themselves apart from the unbelievers. Had we gotten caught, we would have been in serious trouble. Thank goodness they didn't make us sift sand at the hostel. I guess they thought we were too old for that, or closer to the truth, they didn't need sifted sand for building.

This was the year I started dating, but when I say dating, I use the term loosely. One of the hostels, the ELM House, had built a full-size swimming pool, and recreational area above the pool with a bar area and table tennis/darts for their kids. They shared this area with all missionary hostels. Every Friday night, we all went over there for a couple of hours of social time. That was the only real dating time we had. We were never alone. We were always chaperoned and had kids all around us. There were no movie theatres or bowling alleys, or anything else in Jos. We were not allowed to go to the club for Europeans because they sold alcoholic drinks. So the ELM House was it for dates. I began dating John, and Renee was dating Darryl. The four of us were always together. We ate lunch together in our high school cafeteria, a thatched roof hut right outside of our school buildings.

It was fun for a while, but neither Renee nor I were really into our "romantic" relationships. I was still too depressed to give John much of my attention. I know that sounds insensitive, but it is true, and Renee already had a relationship with a British guy who lived in town. So it was really just for fun. They were nice guys. Truth be told, I think the boys felt the same way about the whole thing. But the four of us had a lot of fun with it while it lasted. In fact, at our Spring Prom, which was simply a nice dinner in the school auditorium, we decided to stir things up a bit. I went to the prom with Darryl, and Renee went to the prom with John. What a scandal we caused! There we sat, all four of us at the same table but with different dates! But it was all for laughs, and the next day, we all broke up and stayed good friends for the rest of the year.

It was difficult getting used to living in the hostel. Thirteen girls and three boys for a total of sixteen teenagers that year, all of us third culture kids (TCKs). TCKs are kids who grew up in a culture or cultures different from the culture of their parents for a significant part of their developmental years. So we all shared the challenge that TCKs experience, those same feelings I had when I went to the States for furlough. I didn't fit in the US and I missed my African home when I was on furlough. Birthdays were always hard away from home. I had been at Hillcrest for four weeks, just had my sixteenth birthday at the hostel, and things were pretty busy as I tried to settle into the new school year when my world crumbled. Nigeria had just declared war against Biafra.

Chapter Thirteen

On the Front Line

During the month and year of my sixteenth birthday, September, 1966, thousands of Nigerian people were viciously and pitilessly killed in and around Jos, the city where I lived and attended high school. Not only did I and some of my fellow MKs witness the beatings and killings of Nigerians and Igbos, some of whom we knew and who'd even worked for us, we also knew of rapes, vicious stonings, and public burnings.

We had no access to televisions, and very few of us kids had radios. I received most of my information about the war from the teachers at the high school. We would occasionally have discussions about what was happening at the hostel, but for the most part, our house parents didn't bring up the subject. I think they were trying to protect us, but for me, not knowing caused even more worry.

The missionaries and other expatriates referred to the atrocities as the Biafran conflicts, or the Biafran disturbances, but if you were there in the heart of it, and were honest and objective, to call it a conflict or a disturbance was to belittle or to dismiss what was happening. It was an all-out bloody war. To the Africans, the killings were an important prelude to the Nigerian Civil War of 1967 to 1970, considered one of Africa's most brutal wars. The missionaries mostly chose not to talk about it. They had their own reasons. Some thought that people simply wouldn't be interested. Some had second thoughts that, somehow, they should have gone in and done something more to help. Some felt guilty to varying degrees for whatever happened in more individual situations. Others felt that, as guests in Nigeria, they had to respect what went on with its citizens, and take a backseat to what happened politically.

For us kids, daily life continued, while the chaos churned around us. I wrote about what was happening in my dairy, absorbed it all, until what was going on became my new normal. But it was not normal, and throughout our city of Jos and many other Nigerian towns and villages, on any given day, more than thousands of Igbos were slaughtered trying to flee to their homeland in the eastern region of Biafra.

I love the Nigerian people. They have a spirit of openness and friendliness that is contagious. They are known for their warmth and hospitable nature. And these people came into my life at a time when I needed a sense of security and a loving community. It broke my heart to know they were killing each other, tribe against tribe. Despite my young and naïve understanding of the political situation in Nigeria, I tried to resolve in my own mind how such a seemingly senseless war could occur. I could better understand a war between the Nigerians and the British. Or, more generally speaking, I could have more easily understood a war between the Nigerians and the whites because of white rule in their own country. But fighting each other? All I could see in this godforsaken war was the savage killings of the people I loved. My biggest heartbreak was that I didn't see them as tribes. I saw them as my whole Nigerian family. But of course, that is the view of an outsider, a naïve white outsider at that.

A few times I tried to discuss my feelings with a few of my white friends, but I quickly withdrew when I found out that my thoughts on the matter were quite different from theirs. I was becoming an independent thinker. Our house parents also tended to keep us from the politics of what was going on. And so I further withdrew and a layer of sadness darkened my junior year of high school. Even though I loved being back in Africa, I had just returned from the States and was still missing Maria very much. And maybe it wasn't that my thoughts were so different from my friends' ways of thinking about the war, it was that some of their solutions weren't like mine. I wanted to get out there with the Nigerians and help, hands on. Why couldn't the mission at least speak out? I mean, isn't that why we were out there in the first place? Some of my friends were content to pray, "Let God's will be done." I always thought that sounded like an excuse to do nothing. Not me. Praying wasn't enough. "God helps those who help themselves," I say. Where was this so called God of Love? It was the beginning of a rebellious and confused time in my life.

I hadn't yet resolved my own pain and sadness. I was still resentful and hurt by the breakup of our family and the pain Maria and I had gone through. To see the horrendous slaughtering among the people I had grown to love seemed to fling it all up on a screen and force me to view it in color. My depression and anger grew. I didn't eat and couldn't sleep. I didn't even tell Renee a lot of what was happening. She didn't feel about the Africans and the war the way I did, so I just kept those feelings to myself, while I tried to act as "normal" as possible on the outside. But it was hard to do.

Finally, I reached my limit. I came in from school one afternoon and cut my wrists. Even as I did it, I knew it was a cry for help and not a real attempt to kill myself, but I just didn't know what else to do. I had to make some movement from the state in which I found myself. I just sat on the bed, crying until my roommate came in the room. Sarah called Aunt Pat, who bandaged my wrists. Since I hadn't done any real major damage, she called the doctor to set me up with a visiting mission psychologist.

The mission didn't have a full-time psychologist on staff. If you had problems, you went to the Lord in prayer. I agreed to go to the psychologist only if my parents would not be informed. I didn't want them to worry, and I still felt that obligation to not get in the way of God's work. The psychologist and I talked that afternoon and, I should have known, he called my parents without telling me after our session. Before school the next morning, my parents made a long distance call to the hostel which was a very big deal. Rarely did we get a telephone call in Nigeria. It was very expensive and service was poor. My parents were obviously upset and wanted to know whether or not they should take me back to the States. I knew if that happened, I would forever be known as the one who got in the way of my parents' mission work. I wanted no part of that, so I did a lot of talking to assure them I was fine. I wasn't. I just pretended a lot. I had gotten pretty good at that. Truth be known, I was depressed and lonely.

All of this was going on while the war raged on right in our own neighborhood and town. People would run in mobs of twenty or more carrying machetes, sticks, stones, and knives. You could hear them before you saw them: chanting, grunting, beating drums, yelling, and beating their sticks together. Even from a distance, you could see the looks of hatred and fear on their faces. The Hausa crowd would run recklessly through the road, disregarding cars or people who got in their way, focusing only on the Igbo they were trying to capture. Food stalls, pottery, or anything in their way was destroyed.

All Hillcrest students, and those on the mission compounds, were on curfew. We were not allowed outside after dark, not allowed off our compound without a mission guardian, and had to be shuttled back and forth to school. Our house parent, Uncle Henry, drove us, and occasionally we would see mob beatings. I felt so helpless and sad at these times. Other eye witnesses recounted stories of mobs hacking people to death, cutting them with machetes and knives until their insides fell out. Others witnessed stonings. The mob would throw sticks and stones at an individual until the person would trip or fall and then the mob would close around the individual, and if he or she was an Igbo, would beat the Igbo to death. I witnessed a stoning from a distance and I was struck by this strong desire to run over to the crowd and stop this insanity.

"Uncle Henry," I pleaded, "isn't there anything we can do?"

And in a rare moment of softness he said, "No, if we get any closer, we will be killed ourselves." And I understood but didn't want to believe that these gentle people could be so cruel to each other.

Stores and places belonging to Igbos were looted and then burned. You could see people walking down the street with chairs or other goods on their backs or over their shoulders, taking advantage of the free loot. So many people were killed during this time that the garbage trucks stopped collecting garbage and started going around town collecting dead bodies. These bodies were then buried in huge pits across town.

One Saturday morning in October, Uncle Henry took a few of us into town for supplies and mail pick up. You could tell there was unrest and fear among the local people because everyone was in a hurry. Usually, people would saunter along and talk with each other, share a long greeting, and ask about each other's family and work. Not during these hostile times. People got their business done and hurried home, cautious not to get involved in riots that were prone to pop up at any time. Uncle Henry drove the van cautiously through the crowds. Those of us in the van tried not to stare or draw attention to ourselves. White people were a foreign tribe, and we were all in the way.

As we neared the post office, people crowded the parking lot. As we got closer, Uncle Henry yelled harshly, a tinge of fear in his voice. "Get down! Keep your heads down!"

Before I could duck, the crowd broke, and I saw a large, dark mound. At first, it didn't register what it was. But then my stomach seized. A mound of bodies, twisted dead bodies, were piled in front of the post office. No one should have to see that. No one. Still I wanted to get into the safer places and help out where we could.

Conflicts and disturbances had escalated throughout Nigeria since it gained its independence from British rule in 1960. It was now 1966. Nigeria, like many other African countries, had been artificially formed by the British in the mid-1800s without regard to any concerns of the native peoples' religions, ethnic, tribal, or language differences. Rather, the formation was done to extend the realm of Queen Victoria. To further complicate matters, the British had divided the country into four major populations by tribes: The Hausa mostly in the northern and central part of Nigeria, the Fulani tribes in the North, the Igbos, composed mostly of the Igbo tribes in the Southeast, and the Yoruba, composed mostly of the Yoruba tribes in the Southwestern part of the state.

At the time, the Hausas in the north were the largest group but were a more rural group. The Fulanis were a nomadic tribe.

161

As they were further inland, education and other resources reached these Northern tribes later; therefore, they were not as educated as were the Igbos and Yorubas. The Igbos were an industrious, more educated, and hard-working group of people already living in democratically organized villages. The Yorubas also had a more organized political and social system than tribes in the north and were more educated. This was mainly due to missionary and European influence originally coming in from the coast. The North was mostly Muslim, and the rest of the country was a mix of Islam and Christianity, with the majority still Muslim.

The cause of the war was the attempted secession of the southeastern region of Nigeria which proclaimed itself the Republic of Biafra. Complex underlying causes that involved the ethnic, tribal, and religious differences among these four groups added to the tension among the groups. With the military coup that led to the kidnapping and death of Abubakar Tafawa Belewa, Nigeria's first Prime Minister since its independence, and the counter-coup that led to the brutal death of the Igbo leader, Major-General Johnson Thomas Umunakwe Aguiyi-Ironsi, Nigeria's first military ruler since its independence, tensions were at the highest. The outbreak, and one of the bloodiest days of the war was on September 29, 1966, just weeks after I arrived at Niger Creek, my hostel. There were planned killings of all Igbos across the north, a time when there were systematic eliminations of the Igbos in city after city.

The first coups started on January 15, 1966, when my family and I were on furlough in the States. My parents kept in constant contact with mission headquarters in New York regarding how the political situation was progressing, and whether or not missionaries could or should return. Getting concrete information from the mission was difficult mainly because no accurate information was forthcoming from Nigeria. Coups and riots would pop up throughout Nigeria, but for the most part, we were told that white people would be left alone if they didn't interfere. Apparently, no one except the Igbos were being threatened. I wanted to use the situation as an excuse to stay home and attend my last two years of high school in the

162

States. But there's no way my parents would consider that. They would not leave another "Maria" at the train station.

Upon our return, Africa was a very different place. When we arrived at the airport, we were met with armed guards, guns, and rough personal searches. These were not what missionaries were previously used to, but now we were having them as a way of life. At school, we had a curfew. We could walk to school again, but we had to do it in groups.

A few weeks after school started, I was sitting in Chemistry Lab when I heard the mob right outside of the school's perimeter. When Africans meet in a group, there is usually a musical or rhythmic element involved—drums, chanting, or singing. An African mob utilizes the same elements, only in a different manner. The latter was what I heard off in the distance. It was a low, almost guttural expulsion of sound and air resulting in a grunt-like sound, loud, slow, very steady, and constant. It was a fearful sound, a powerful sound, a dangerous sound. A sound I felt deep within me.

Our small high school was a string of classrooms connected by a covered breezeway. Without warning, a young Igbo boy ran into the open door of our classroom. The mob was Hausa and the boy, an Igbo. He was our Chemistry teacher's steward or house boy. The students were frozen with fright. We knew our lives were in danger. Mr. Keipers, our Chemistry teacher, sprang into action as his steward cried out: "Masta, Masta, hep me, hep me, I beg! Masta, hep me. De go beat me. Dis da I die. Ples, masta, I beg. Hep me." He was speaking of the Hausa mob closing in behind him.

The same broken English accent that we MKs often mimicked in a lighthearted way, I heard this time in a much different light. The house boy was speaking those words for his own survival. And I was thinking almost the same words for my own survival. "God, Oh God, help me, please, I beg you. Don't let this mob beat me to death and kill me. I do try to be a good MK. I don't mean to be this way. I really try, but it's all just so hard. Why do you have to be so cruel anyway?" This was the common thread of all my prayers during the days of those riots as the war continued.

Mr. Keipers' eyes darted around the room and with the approaching mob now on school grounds, shoved the young man into the storage compartment under his demonstration table and shut the cabinet door. The young boy was covered scrapes and bruises. He had been either beaten and gotten away or had at least hurt himself trying to get away from the mob. The smell of abject terror and the boy's sweat filled the air.

Mr. Weaver, our principal, had also seen and heard the mob, and had already called the military police. We were shocked that they showed up and were able to temporarily avert the mob. At least for a while, the young Igbo was safe. We were all safe. When the mob was gone, Mr. Keipers pulled his shaken steward out from under the cabinet and took him outside. Our teacher did not tell us what he told his steward or what eventually happened to him.

One thing I do recall from the aftermath of that incident was the headache which I had. It was the worst headache of my life. I was in fear from the excruciating pain. Aunt Pat said it was probably a migraine from the stress of what happened. She gave me a two Tylenol and told me to take one now and take the other one only if I needed it in about four hours. She said they were very strong. I had taken Tylenol many times before, and I never thought they were very strong. What did Aunt Pat know? So I took both of them. She hadn't told me they were Tylenol *with codeine.*

I lay there on my bed, my special goose feather pillow over my head, and after about twenty-five minutes, I felt a warm feeling in my chest. It was a new sensation. I liked it. I paid attention to it and forgot about my headache. Ten minutes later, the feeling had spread throughout my entire body, and I felt a sensation of warmth and numbness. The numbness was similar to when I used to spin and "go away," but the warmth and tingling added a whole new dimension. I was feeling great. Not only was I feeling no pain, I was downright happy! Either I had been filled by the Holy Ghost or it was those pills! And since the Holy Ghost and I weren't on such good terms, I decided it was the pills. From that moment, I plotted how I could obtain some more. For the first time in years, I had no worries, in spite of my dulled, now almost non-existent headache, in spite of my being in the hostel, and in spite of the war going on around me. I was experiencing a beautiful calmness, something I could never remember feeling. I had never felt this good before, and I wanted to feel it again.

The actual Nigerian Civil War didn't begin until a few months later, on July 6, 1967. It ended January 13, 1970. By that time, I had graduated from Hillcrest and gone back to the States. Once the purge had been completed, and there were no more Igbos in the North where I had been living, things quieted down. We heard about the war, which was being fought mostly in the South and Southeast of Nigeria, but aside from a small skirmish here and there, life in the North went on pretty much as normal. However, during this time, thousands and thousands of Biafrans (also called Igbos) were being killed and starved to death in the East.

The Biafran War was one of the first African conflicts receiving such widespread attention that led to the formation of humanitarian organizations that would respond to similar emergencies all around the world. I was used to seeing malnourished children running around in some of the villages with runny noses and grossly swollen bellies, but nothing prepared me for the pictures I saw of the starving children of Biafra. There was a name for it: *kwashi-*

The malnourished children scrounging for food.

orkor. This was a form of malnutrition caused by the chronic loss of protein and other necessary nutrients that the body needs. The symptoms are apathy, weakness and fatigue, thinning hair, loss of teeth, and grossly swollen stomachs due to the swelling of the liver. The blockades the Nigerian government placed around Biafra made it almost impossible for the humanitarian aid groups to get food and supplies into the province.

I vividly remember the mobs chasing after Igbos, their machetes and knives raised, the rocks being thrown, the mound of bodies in front of the post office, and the look of terror in the steward's eyes as he begged for help. I still hear the cries for help and the angry shouts of the mobs, the chanting so different from the usual happy chants, singing, and music. If you have never seen war up close, if you have never seen one human intentionally hurt or killed by another human being, it is easy to make light of war. People even pay money to be entertained by watching it. But once death and war have touched you personally, you know that it is inconceivable what we as humans will do to each other in the name of God, or country, or any other ideal. Let it never be so.

The Biafran war was a great sadness for me. It came at a vulnerable time in my life. I love Africa and its people. And to see them fighting against each other so viciously when all I had known them to be were a kind and generous people was most disheartening. I wanted to help. I wanted to be down there with my classmates from the other missions helping the wounded and dying. But for whatever reasons, our mission chose not to let us get involved because my mission chose not to get involved. They felt it best to stay out of Nigeria's politics because they said they were guests in their country. I felt confused. I felt at the end of my rope. I was under the impression they were missionaries, called by God to minister, help and heal. I must have been wrong. I must have misunderstood this whole "missions" thing.

Smile

Smile though your heart is aching
Smile even though it's breaking.
When there are clouds in the sky
you'll get by if you smile through
*   your fear and sorrow*
Smile and maybe tomorrow
You'll see the sun come shining through
for you.

Light up your face with gladness,
Hide every trace of sadness.
Although a tear may be ever so near.

That's the time you must keep on trying
Smile, what's the use of crying.
You'll find that life is still worthwhile
if you just smile.

You'll find that life is still worthwhile
if you just smile.

Lyrics by John Turner
and Geoffrey Parsons

Chapter Fourteen

She'll Never Amount to Anything?

Summer break at Ilorin was short and sweet, only six weeks. I spent most days at the club listening to tunes, soaking up rays, and eating chips drowned in malt vinegar. I would even order an alcoholic drink if I had enough money. A vodka fruit drink was my favorite. I had learned how to drink alcohol in eleventh grade. Renee and I had made friends with some of the kids at Hillcrest who lived in town. On rare occasions, we would sneak out, go visit them, and have a few drinks. I hated the taste of alcohol, but I loved the feeling it gave me. It was almost as good as the codeine. Life was now bearable.

Edward and Ann were home from KA, and they sure were growing up fast. Ann and I shared a room together, and I really enjoyed lying in bed at night talking to her. I really missed both of them the past year while I was at Hillcrest.

The twins and I tended to the rabbits that my Dad raised for food in Ilorin and occasionally sold or gave away some to anyone interested. There were about ten or twelve cages to take care of each day. My sister had her two pet monkeys, Fredricka and *Soho* (Old Man). She used to sit in their cage and

One of Ann's (two) pet monkeys, Soho or Fredricka. I can't tell the two apart.

let them groom her hair. I tried it a few times, but the whole procedure gave me the willies. I fully expected to get lice, maggots, or some other such nasty parasite from them. But they were so cute.

My brother had a pet rooster. This rooster was the biggest rooster I had ever seen, and being a country girl, I have seen plenty of roosters. He was also beautiful. He had a shiny set of

Edward's pet rooster.

rust-colored feathers that reflected the sun, and a tall, erect comb that was as red as a sun-kissed apple. Edward would walk around the yard with this behemoth in his arms as if it was his baby. Me? I shared our dachshund, Prince, with everyone in the family. He was a most terrific dog! The Africans thought it amusing that we kept animals as pets, loved them as family members, fed them and kept them in our homes, while it was their custom to eat all of them, even the dogs.

Sometimes during the rainy season, usually in the late afternoon or at night, we would be visited by huge swarms of flying ants. From trees, holes in the ground, or their favorite, cracks in the patio or pavement, the up to inch long black ants emerged by the thousands. It was the nuptial flight to make a nest for their queen. Some nests could have up to 20,000 workers. These rather fat and juicy ants could have even longer, transparent wings.

One late afternoon, as the usual afternoon shower was winding down, I heard a commotion at our front door. As I ran to the door, I saw two Nigerian girls about my age sitting on our front steps talking and giggling excitedly. I had seen them around a lot, but I didn't know them by name. I discovered that they lived in our staff housing with their parents. As I got closer, I saw that one of them held a large open bowl full of water. I stepped outside on the porch, greeting them in Hausa.

"Sannu," I said.

"Yauwa, Sannu," each girl said back, between giggles.

It was then that I saw the winged ants. Thousands of them were coming out of a crack in the bottom of the foundation between our house and porch. As fast as they were coming out, the girls began scooping them up with their hands and then forcefully throwing them into the bowl of water. When their wings hit the water, the ants would stick to the water's surface and they could not escape.

"Ach! Ach! *Menene?*" (What is this?) Hoping I had said the right thing in Hausa.

"It iss de Day of Ants and it iss ouwa dinna," replied one of the girls.

Great! She spoke English. In most Nigerian schools, they speak English from an early age. I was running out of Hausa words.

"Your dinner? Are you going to eat these ants?" I tried not to sound surprised so I wouldn't offend them.

"Oh yes, miss. De taste iss vedy, vedy gud." During our conversation, I had started helping the girls catch the ants. The ants kept coming, and the three of us kept scooping them up and throwing them into the water. One of the girls kept taking the bowl back to her house to empty it, returning with a clean bowl full of water.

Me standing inside the glass door watching the ants coming up from inside the ground.

Once, while we were waiting, I asked the girl with me her name. She said it was Lydia. Many Christian Africans name their children after a name from the Bible. I said Lydia was a beautiful name. She dropped her head and said shyly,

Me watching Lydia preparing the grease to fry the ants.

"Na gode" (thank you). I liked her immediately.

"Lydia, since you got the ants from my porch, may I come with you and watch you cook them, and maybe eat some of them as well?"

"Eh (yes), dis will be vedy gud. Let us go now. We haf plenty ants." We took the last bowl of ants and went over to her house to prepare them. Her sister, Martha, was already heating oil over

Edward is sampling the fried ants, no hesitation on his part.

an outside fire. As soon as Lydia and I got there, Lydia filled the pot of boiling oil with ants. Immediately, the wings disintegrated, and the ants turned crispy. With trepidation, I tried one and found they were really not bad. They reminded me of little pieces of crispy fried chicken. We sat around the fire, ate flying ants, and talked into the evening.

I made two new friends that day. They had black skin. I had white skin. They spoke Hausa. I spoke English. But after a few hours of Lydia and Martha helping me with my Hausa, and me helping them with their English, as well as sharing food together, we found out we were basically the same underneath. How delightful!

It was a great six-week break, but once again, it was time to go back to school, this time as a senior. I was looking forward to my last year at Hillcrest. I was not looking forward to leaving Africa. I had gotten to know several of the American Peace Corps (APC) workers at the club in Ilorin, and they tried to recruit me to the Peace Corps. I thought it would be a great idea to get my nursing degree and then return to Africa as an APC worker. Of course, Mother's plans for me were to return as a missionary nurse, something I knew I would never do, not after my experiences with the mission.

I started school in August. The twins didn't start until September, so once again, I flew up alone. By now, I was a veteran to flying—no air-sickness, no nausea, no tears, no loneliness, *no feelings, nothing.*

I got to school the day before school started, and I had a lot to do to get ready. I wasn't too happy with my hostel room location. It was on the same side of the hostel as was Uncle Henry and Aunt Pat's living quarters, and unfortunately, right across the hall from their personal living room. On the other hand, my room was also across the hall from the medicine closet, the closet where the Tylenol with codeine was kept. I had become quite adept at sneaking a few at a time out of the big pharmacy size canister. So, that was convenient. I ended up with two great roommates, and the depression I had been plagued with had subsided somewhat. I had high hopes for a good year.

My senior classes were a little more difficult, but the schedule and routine were very much the same. I played a lot of field hockey on the hot dusty field, but it was a great way to get rid of aggression and loneliness. My classes included Shorthand, Home Economics, Typing, Biology II, and other basic subjects. The Shorthand was a waste of time; I already knew most everything that was offered in Home Economics, thanks to Mother; but the Typing was extremely helpful when I started nursing school the next year. I used to go in after school to practice on the school typewriters.

I thought back on my year on furlough at Towers High—about all the fun things that American kids did, not bad things, just normal fun, teenage things. And I wondered why our MK lives had to be so restricted. Why did we have so many rules placed on us? Why we were watched so closely, as if we would do something wrong if left alone? It had been that way since we first came to KA, all the way through high school.

I had been dating a nice guy, Jerry, for several months. Jerry was walking me home from school one day, with permission, and we stopped in one of the Hillcrest teacher's houses that was under construction. It was barely framed up and nothing had been placed in it so we decided to go take a look. We stepped up into the house and walked around. Right before we left the house to go on to the hostel, Jerry pulled me behind one of the walls and gave me a big, long kiss. I was so excited because we had only gotten an opportunity like that once before. We were just pulling away from each other when Miss Taylor, whose house it was to be, showed her head around the corner.

"What are you two doing here? This is my house," she said.

"We didn't know this was your house. We were just looking around," said Jerry.

"Looks to me you were doing a lot more than looking around." Then she started preaching to us about the sins of teen sex. I knew she hadn't seen anything, because we hadn't done anything, but we couldn't convince her of that. We had sinned in her eyes and in the eyes of God, when in fact we were acting like normal teenage kids. She continued preaching and belittling us and said that I had to come to her office the next day and have another talk with her. Then, in front of Jerry, she looked at me and said: "Girls like you never amount to anything!"

I turned around and ran back to the hostel, without saying a word to Jerry or Miss Taylor. I wasn't supposed to be out by myself, but I didn't care. Jerry later told me that he tried to catch me as I ran back to the hostel, but I didn't hear him because I was crying. I was so hurt, humiliated, and angry at what Miss Taylor said. I knew in my soul that I had done nothing wrong. I snuck in the back door; Aunt Pat was preparing dinner in the kitchen, and Uncle Henry was out in the backyard. I went straight to the medicine closet, opened the pharmacy size canister of Tylenol with codeine, and grabbed both hands full of pills. I took them back to my room. After taking four pills, thinking it just might end it all, I hid the rest.

I went to the kitchen and told Aunt Pat I had a sandwich on the way home, and I didn't feel good. I told her that I was going to go to bed early. She tried to talk me out of it, but she finally said okay. Back in my room, I started feeling that warm feeling the codeine always offered to me. Once in my PJ's, I crawled in bed and "went away" in my mind. I was wild with anger and told myself I had been abused in any manner for the last time. I was not going to take it anymore. I would not let it bother me, I *could* not let it bother me. It was too painful, too wrenching. The drugs were now hitting me hard. I lay still and let them take me to a place where I could be me. I didn't have to pretend to be good, or godly, or anything. Just me. Just me.

"Cheryl, Cheryl. Wake up! You've already missed breakfast, and it's just about time to get on the van. You've been asleep since before dinner last night. What's wrong with you?" asked my roommate, Sandy, quite alarmed.

My first thought as I awoke was that I was alive. Then, as if it didn't matter, I jumped up and ran for the bathroom. On the way, I nearly passed out and stumbled, but I recovered. A hot shower cleared my head. The only side effects—hunger.

When we arrived at the school, the first thing I did was head for Miss Taylor's office as she had requested. I had about ten minutes before the bell was going to ring for classes. For the entire time, she blamed me for what happened. She told me that I had tempted Jerry. She said I was one of those slut girls. She gave me statistics on teen pregnancy; but the one thing she tried to drill in my head was that it was always the girl's responsibility to not let things like this happen. *Things like what?* I asked myself. I hadn't done anything. She stressed that if anything happened, it was always the girl's fault. I totally disagreed with her philosophy, but I didn't say anything and kept my anger bottled up inside. The first bell rang, and I heard her say to herself out loud as I ran out the door, "She'll never amount to anything." Her remarks cut deep. I knew how to deal with those feelings of craziness and depression. I popped two codeine tablets, angry at myself for feeling shamed.

I don't know if anyone else at the hostel had found out the secret about the codeine pills and had also been helping themselves; but apparently my abundant handfuls had made an obvious dent in the pill supply, and Aunt Pat figured there were mice in the medicine cupboard. She moved the good stuff to a hidden location, and I had been cut off. I had a few hidden away, but I had become mentally/emotionally dependent on them.

I had taken the SAT test earlier in the year and had made a little above average scores. I managed an average of B- all during high school. I was a little nervous when I filled out my application forms for the Nursing School at Georgia Baptist Hospital

(GBH), a three-year nursing school, where I was hoping to obtain a degree as Registered Nurse. I finally received the letter of acceptance from GBH. Going away to college began to feel real to me. It was only a matter of weeks before I would be leaving my home in Africa. All that was left was graduation.

The Graduation Ceremony was held on Tuesday, June 11, 1968, at 7:30 p.m. in the school auditorium. It felt strange to have my parents and brother and sister there at the school with me. I had nothing to compare it to, this being the first graduation program I had ever attended, but I thought it was nice enough. It started with *Exultate Jubilate* by Mozart, followed by the processional which was a selection from *Tannhauser* by Wagner. This was performed by our high school orchestra. We had the Welcome and a few prayers, the introduction of the speaker by his son who was in our class, then the address by his father. Next came the presentation of the diplomas, all eighteen! I reached out my left hand to receive my diploma and to shake the principal's hand with my right. As I left the stage, I felt a tremendous sense of relief. I realized I had survived quite a bit since my first arrival in Africa: the sense of abandonment, the abuse, the loneliness, the riots, and the religious hypocrisy. Some of my coping mechanisms may not have been ideal, but they got me through the tough times. It was a little daunting to think about going back to and living on my own, but I had been on my own emotionally for so long, it wouldn't be new to me.

My parents had been begging me to spend the summer in Ilorin with them. But I was in a hurry to get back to the States. I am not sure why I felt such a rush. I liked living in Ilorin. I guess I felt a need to get back and start my life away from the influence of the mission.

Chapter Fifteen
Going Home or Leaving Home?

For the next week, my family and I spent our time in and around the Jos Guest House. Mom and I shopped a little for African curios to take back as gifts to our family, but mostly I spent time together with my parents and the twins. I knew it would be two years before I saw them again.

It was strange. People would ask me if I was excited about going home. I would stop and think. Home? I was excited about going back to the States, but I did not have the feeling that I was going back home. I had no actual home that I was going back to in Georgia. In fact, I was going to be living with an older, childless couple I had never met, and we would be living across town in an area with which I was unfamiliar.

I had more of a feeling that I was leaving home. It was not about one particular place that we had lived; it was leaving Africa itself. Over the years I had been in this magical place, I had the privilege to befriend all of those wonderful Africans, lived in those many different spots, taken in all the beauty the country had to offer. I gradually absorbed bits and parts of Africa into me. I actually felt like I was part African inside, and I was proud of it. So, although I was eager to get back to the States for college, I knew in my heart that someday I would go back to Africa.

The night before I was to leave, Dad was quiet, subdued. I used to describe him as quiet sometimes, but as I got older, I realized he suffered from migraine headaches and depression. Dad and I sat and talked for a while before we all went to bed. I knew he was sad that I wasn't staying with them for the summer, but I knew that it wasn't the right thing for me at that time. What

I really wanted to ask my parents was whether or not they would come home with me where we could all live as a family. I knew the answer. They wouldn't. They had been called by God and would stay true to that calling unless "lead" by Him to do otherwise.

I woke after a restless night. My flight to Kano was leaving that morning, and I had some last minute packing to do before we left for the airport. I would be flying the entire trip to New York with another missionary family. They had four children, and with the two parents we counted seven in all. We looked like a bunch of gypsies, which is what most missionaries looked like after four years in Africa: homemade clothes, funny hair styles, Bata shoes, basically ten to fifteen years behind the times. After having prayer time and saying our goodbyes as a family, we left for the airport. I noticed myself fighting back the tears. I didn't want to further upset Dad. As it was, I knew he would go into a tailspin as soon as I left. So I hardened myself. I tightened my body. I didn't breathe for long stretches. I tried not to think about leaving my family. I knew once I was on the plane, I could "go away," and feel only numbness.

During my years in Africa, I came to realize it was the departures and arrivals, the leaving and the coming back, that are some of the hardest times for the missionary child. I hugged my family tight. With one last look and wave, I got into the plane, and headed to Kano. Like my sister, I would be married when I next saw my parents.

The rest of the trip was pretty much a blur. We stopped over in a couple of countries to sightsee. I woke up in Italy to find out my one and only suitcase had been misplaced by the airlines. With nothing but what I had on to wear, I had to borrow one of the other girl's clothes. She was the same size as me but in fifth grade. I was mortified. The clothes were obviously for a little girl. I didn't want to be seen in public anywhere. But when I arrived in New York, amazingly, there was my suitcase!

In New York, at the old Mission Home, I had a whole day to myself before flying on to Atlanta. So I went shopping.

I found the directions to Macy's downtown. I took off, walking by myself, straight out of the sticks in Africa to downtown

Manhattan. I was halfway there and began to wonder if this was a wise idea. I wasn't expecting to see the number of homeless people. It was my first exposure to communities of hippies. I found them fascinating and was drawn to them. My feet were killing me, and I thought I should have been there by now. But I persevered, until I saw the big Macy's sign. It was huge and magnificent. I can't remember ever seeing a store that big. I knew exactly what I wanted to purchase, so I hurried right in and straight to the makeup counter. I waited forever for some assistance and finally had to ask for some help. I was surprised at how rude the salesperson spoke to me, but I wasn't going to let that ruin my fun. I bought some Shiseido makeup, powder, mascara, eye liner, and lipstick. I had no idea that makeup could be that expensive, and I forgot to ask the price before she rang it all up and put it in the bag.

"That will be $96 even," she said, nicely this time.

"Oh! Uh, Okay, thank you," I said, feeling sick. Dad had given me some money before I left, but I couldn't keep spending it like this or it wouldn't last long. And he had reminded me that I couldn't *chiniki* (bargain) in American stores, so I didn't even try. In the back of my mind I remember one of the uncles warning me I would suffer from culture shock and to look out for it and be prepared. In hindsight, it was a good warning.

Next, I went to the Ladies' dress department, where I bought a baby blue shift with white trim, similar to the one I had made for starting tenth grade when I was home on furlough, but there was nothing handmade or cheap about this one. I didn't know anything about ladies or teen sizes: a five, seven, nine, or a two, four, six. I just looked for the dress I liked and hoped it fit. I tried it on and it fit like a glove and was very stylish. I loved that dress. It was shorter than would be allowed at Hillcrest but it wasn't a mini dress. Of course, the dress had to have some high heels. White patent leather, I thought, and a new bag to match. My snakeskin African bag just didn't look right with the outfit! At least I wouldn't look like a gypsy when Maria picked me up at the airport in Atlanta.

I took a taxi back to the Mission and barely made it back before dark. I couldn't believe how many shopping bags I had collected. One of the staff members at the mission had told me at breakfast that I had to be back before dark as I was not allowed out in the city by myself. When I got back to my room, I carefully laid my new dress out on an old wooden straight-back chair, put my new shoes under the chair, changed purses, and laid out everything else I would need for the next day. I was so excited about seeing my sister and her husband, I doubted that I would sleep a wink. I even skipped dinner.

I had a morning flight on Delta to Atlanta, but I was ready to go well before breakfast. I began reading the book I bought to take on the flight. The missionary who ran the mission took me to the airport and helped me to the plane. I thanked him, but as I got on, I felt grateful to be through with the mission: through with their rules, their beliefs that put God before family, and their hypocrisy.

As I was boarding the plane, I noticed it was a jet. This was my first flight on a real jet, and I couldn't believe my luck. Heretofore, I had been flying propeller or prop-jet planes; and I was so excited to see what it would be like to fly in a real jet. But in spite of my excitement, or maybe because of it, I found myself crying on the plane. I didn't understand if it was from happiness or sadness. I was one confused young lady. So much had happened the last few days. I would be calling Mother and Dad tonight to let them know I arrived safely and was with Maria. The jet ride was everything I was hoping it would be, especially the speed and power of the take-off and the deceleration power of the landing. It was a nice June summer day in Atlanta.

I carefully followed the people on my flight through the airport until I collected my bag in Baggage Claim. Then I continued on through the crowds, and there she was, Maria. I hugged her tight, crying like a baby, forgetting that my makeup would run all down my cheeks. We had a laugh about that, and everything was good again.

I stayed with Maria and Allen for a week. But things were different with them now. They were new parents, with a new baby boy. Mother had arranged for me to stay with an older couple from the church that took in missionary kids in need of a home. Sound familiar? I had never met them before, but I thought

I could put up with anything or anybody until I started school in September. They were seemingly nice enough, but very set in their ways. You definitely knew you were a guest in their home, and as such I knew their rules must be obeyed. By their mannerisms, I always felt my stay was temporary, and I never felt comfortable in their home, even though they gave me "my own room." It wouldn't matter too much, I would only be there during summer, Christmas, and some weekends, because I would be living in the dormitory during the three years at GBH, just like KA and Hillcrest. Still, I wasn't too happy about going right into another strange home and away to another boarding school.

It occurred to me that my life was taking a turn very similar to my older sister's when she was left at the train station. She was abandoned by my parents, left with a strange church family for four years with people she did not know, and she had to fend for herself. She was fifteen; I was seventeen—only two years older. I was destined to become a missionary nurse, sent to a religious nursing school, would live with a church couple I had never met, while the rest of my family stayed in Africa for another two years. But that's not quite how my life played out, thank goodness.

It was June when I arrived in the States, and about three weeks after I was home, I was visiting my (*real*) aunt, uncle, and two cousins, and I went to church with them on Sunday morning. It just so happened that I saw a really cute guy in the congregation on the other side of the church, and I let him know I was interested in him with my eyes. It turns out that my cousin knew him as they both went to the same college for the summer. The next day, they ran into each other in the college parking lot.

"Hi, James! You had a cute girl with you yesterday at church," said the cute guy, whose name turned out to be Ken.

"That wasn't my girlfriend, that was my cousin," James replied.

"Sweets!" Ken replied, visibly relieved. "Can I get her phone number?"

He did and called me up. By this time, I was living with the Millers. As soon as I moved in, they thought I needed to get a job, so they helped me get one at Six Flags over Georgia. It was the first year they opened. For our first semi-blind date, Ken picked me up after work one night. We went to see *Where Were You When the Lights Went Out.* It truly was love at first sight, and we dated through the summer. Then I started nursing school.

By then it was quite obvious to others that Ken and I were serious about each other, and the Millers didn't approve. They didn't want anything to interfere with my school, and they felt responsible for me since my parents were still in Africa, and I was still in the Georgia Baptist School of Nursing.

One Friday afternoon in the fall, I left the school to spend the weekend at the Miller's house. As I came up the winding drive, I saw about six or seven boxes on the front porch, including my suitcase. I got out of the car and went to the front door. The side door I usually go into was locked. I rang the doorbell after finding the front door locked as well. This was very unusual as they were always at home when I was supposed to be there. Then I looked down at the boxes and realized to my confusion, they held all of my belongings. Everything I owned was sitting on the front porch in boxes. The house was locked. No one was in the house. I had been shut out. Why? I had no earthly idea. What had I done to deserve this? The hurt was paralyzing. I was sitting on the top step, no one around, and I didn't know what to do. I had nowhere to go. Finally, I pulled myself together.

Ken and I had planned to get together that afternoon and he would be there in about an hour. So I just waited. And sure enough, he arrived on time. I ran to him and threw my arms around him before he even had a chance to get out of the car. Through my sobbing, I told him what had happened. In his quiet and gentle way, he held me tight, assured me that everything would be alright, and didn't let me go until I had calmed myself. Then we placed the boxes in his car and left the Miller's house. That would be the last time I would ever go there.

I lived with Maria during the weekends and holidays. Not ideal, but it worked for a while. Ken and I were engaged nine months after I left Africa. And nine months later, on December 27, 1969, we were married.

We had two beautiful sons, and I wondered to myself how anyone could send their children away to a boarding school hundreds of miles away, in a strange land, to be raised by strangers. It was inconceivable to me. And yet my own parents had made that decision. Not all MKs have negative experiences, thankfully, but I suffered sustained childhood trauma. And, I developed coping methods from an early age that were effective but also detrimental to me. These coping methods included "going away," as I called it, splitting, denying my feelings and what was happening around me, and, as I would find out later in life, repression. Most of these behaviors stayed with me throughout my life. My adult life was full of addictions that began with my spinning as well. But through therapy and prayer, I am a whole person now. I live free and happy. My Dad has passed, and I have a wonderful relationship with my dear Mother who is ninety-two and running circles around me! I also have a new concept of God. No longer is He the God of Judgement that I was taught as a child, the God that my parents and the mission taught me about. I now experience Him differently. For the first time, I can say His name with love and respect. And I thank Him for helping me get through the aftermath of my life as a MK.

A Blessing from Our Father

May the Father bless you with a growing assurance of His great love for you.

May His grace and mercy fill you with unending peace.

May your heart continually grow tender to the Spirit's leading, and

May you rest in the truth that He works all things together for good.

In seasons of adversity and pain,

May you be overwhelmed by His presence and protection, and

May the companions of health and wisdom be yours in abundance.

Epilogue

Ken, my husband of many years, and I are sipping coffee in a restaurant on the eighteenth floor of a hotel that overlooks the Forbidden City in Beijing, China. Our cell phones buzz as we excitedly recount our six-mile hike on The Great Wall to family back home. This trip marks the fifty-third country I have been lucky enough to visit thanks to the travel bug living in Africa gave me. We have gone on many others through Ken's business. Our two sons have travelled with us on many of these trips as well as on their own; so travelling has been our family hobby for many years now. It has given us all a broader world view and a more open perspective on life.

I didn't realize until I was older how much Africa would change me. So much about living in Africa was a satisfying quench for my thirsty senses. Never since have I found another place that stimulated me the way Africa does. I will be forever be grateful to the people of Nigeria for awakening in me the joy of experiencing the cultures and spirit of exploration that I have so enjoyed in my travels.

But living in Africa was not all beautiful sunsets. Though I am sure there are many MKs who had positive experiences during their years in Africa, I and many others were unhappy both at school and at our homes. Tragically, physical, verbal, and even sexual abuse was viewed with a blind eye like we have learned was the case in the Catholic church and other religious environments. At least during the years I was an MK in Africa, children came second to doing the work of God on the mission field. That was the reason my parents left Maria, my sister, back home in the States, tearing apart our family. I have no idea what it was like for her those years we were separated. I only know pieces from here and there. She has never spoken openly to me about it, even though I have asked.

I do know that my brother and sisters and I had no input into my parents' choice to go to Africa as missionaries. We did not choose to be uprooted from our homes. We did not choose to move so many times. We did not choose to go on furlough and lose our friends. We did not choose to suffer from culture shock, to be parented by aunties and uncles, or strangers from the church. I certainly did not choose to be sexually abused. A fellow MK wrote so meaningfully in her blog, "All these decisions were made for us by parents and mission personnel who chose to sacrifice their children for missionary work." *Is that what God wanted? Was that His will?* the child within asks. But it is the wounded child that must heal, while the parents get the praises for serving God.

In the end, I survived. I even grew to be stronger and more resilient because of my struggles. Along the way, I felt bitterness and anger. Addictions suppressed my hurt and loneliness. But I learned to forgive and to embrace compassion for those who had been hurt and even for those who had hurt me. And finally, I learned to forgive myself, care for myself, even *love myself*, which was the greatest lesson and gift of all.

As an adult, I have a better understanding of my parents' decision to become missionaries and move to Africa. I have talked with them about it a few times while we were on furlough, and in more recent years, after some of the anger passed. They were conservative Christians for most of their adult lives. They had a "calling" from God to go to the mission field. They felt it was the right thing to do. They knew there would be sacrifices. But they thought they would be the ones sacrificing, never thinking it would be their children that would be sacrificed. Maria and I were not part of their decision, but we trusted them that we would be safe and everything would be alright. But everything wasn't.

Over my years in Africa, I witnessed first-hand a lot of wonderful and inspirational work done by missionaries and others to help the African people. This included doctors and nurses who performed eye surgery and provided medical support, and helped eradicate leprosy and polio. It included many kind and caring individuals who taught English and business education to help create jobs, to build youth centers, reservoirs, and water purification systems. And this was good.

While Africa is always in my soul, I have made many wonderful friends along the way, have two wonderful sons and a daughter-in-law, two of the most wonderful gifts—my precious grandsons, and my loving husband. Most important, I now believe in a loving God, not the judgmental God I was taught about in Africa. I learned of my loving God much later in life. I had grown up believing that as long as I pleased others and did what they wanted me to do, they would like me. I earned a Ph.D. in Psychology, trying to impress, to understand, to elicit approval. Now, I let my loving God fill the hole of emptiness. I am on a journey of another kind, not to another country, but one in which I am traveling from emptiness to well-being.

And I am a child of the most-high God.

It's not the destination; it's the journey.

Acknowledgements

I contemplated many years about writing this memoir. I didn't want to dredge up old memories: I didn't want to hurt anyone's feelings. I feared I wouldn't be able to remember enough details to fill a book and had other excuses about writing this book. But thankfully, there were enough people in my life who encouraged and helped me to continue my dream of writing my story, not only for my own good but also because we believed it was a story worth telling.

TO KEN, MY LOVING HUSBAND: This book would not have been possible except for the loving support and encouragement from you. From the very start, when I had doubts, you challenged me and convinced me that this book was a worthy cause. When the hurtful, old memories seemed overwhelming, your unconditional love gave me the warmth and security that I needed to continue. You were my tech man and so much more. I am so glad that we will continue as always, teammates for over four decades.

MY FAMILY: Writing a book of this nature brings up old memories; for me it was a lot of painful memories, ones I had worked hard to resolve with my therapist and then to forget. So I wasn't in the best of spirits during the writing of this book, and I am most grateful to my loving husband, Ken, and my two sons, Stephen and Mark, and Mark's wife, Megan, for their enduring love and patient support, throughout the writing years. I felt their love and compassion when it was needed most. Thanks, guys. Not to forget my two grandsons, Miles and Max; you are loved more than you know and you give me such joy and happiness.

Ken, thanks for the hugs and encouragement when the times were especially tough. You've been there for me since the Miller's kicked me out. I love you forever and a day.

GRACE MICHAEL: Grace is my Editor-at-Large. She is a consummate professional, providing essential guidance as well as final editing and page layout and design that included sharing her wisdom gained over her many years of publishing experience. I would never have maneuvered the final stages of publishing my memoir without her superb support. Grace, thank you for your patience, speed, and thoughtful expertise in helping to make this a successful book.

THOMAS OWEN DUVALL, JD: Thomas Owen Duvall, JD, Attorney at Law, my dear brother-in-law and friend, I want to thank you for not only encouraging me along this writing journey but also for being my informal attorney to answer any legal questions keeping me out of trouble. In spite of your own hardships these past few years, you have always had a joke and a smile for us. My love and thanks.

KATY TAYLOR: I owe a big debt of gratitude to Katy Taylor, my friend and early editor. This is my first attempt of writing non-academic material, and you took my first draft and turned it into something almost enjoyable to read! You didn't laugh at what I had written, you even encouraged me to keep going. Thank you for your professionalism, your friendship, and your love.

DR. TRUETT GANNON: One of the most important men in my life, besides my husband, is Dr. Truett Gannon, Professor of Theology, Mercer University, Atlanta Campus; and retired Pastor of Smoke Rise Baptist Church, Stone Mountain, Georgia. He taught me, by the way he lived and through the words he spoke, that the God of my childhood was not the true, loving God. Through his gentle, patient guidance I began to reconnect with people; and he paved the way for me to believe that I truly could have a different relationship with God. Thank you, Truett, for being there, for me and for my family.

No two people have been more influential helping me overcome some of my deep-seated fears and needs to escape reality than psychotherapist and published author, Bernie Schein and psychiatrist, Dr. Thomas W. Bantly, MD.

BERNIE SCHEIN: Author of *If Holden Caulfield Were in My Classroom, Famous All Over Town,* and *Pat Conroy: Our Life-long Friendship,* Bernie had a tricky light hearted and somewhat unorthodox manner that I found very effective in my early awakenings and growth. To me, his style of therapy was blunt, face-to-face, physical, sensitive, and compassionate; most of all, to the point and honest. You couldn't pull one on Bernie (believe me, I tried in the early days). Thanks for persisting, Bernie!

DR. THOMAS BANTLY: Dr. Bantly, quite the opposite of Bernie, is much more structured. I found him very compelling and what I needed at that time in my growth. I liked him immediately and have grown to trust him through the years. I credit him with integrating all those alternate "me's" I needed so desperately earlier in life, with the "me" I am learning to love— Cheryl—one and the same. He is well-known and well-respected, and now retired from practice in Snellville, Georgia. I will miss you so much. Thank you, Dr. Bantly.

CAROLYN LORENZ: I would like to give my best friend a hug of thanks for what she has meant to me. I met Carolyn when I was ten years old and our friendship continues until this day. She was the first friend I made when I arrived in Lagos, and our friendship continued through high school, and through our adulthood. Thanks for your comments in making this a better book, but most of all, thanks for being my lifelong friend. You are truly a soul-mate.

FRIENDS: I have been very blessed to have had many special friends in my life—friends that are lovers of life, and loved nothing more than to share many hours of conversations on how to make life more meaningful. Through the years, these times together have been significant to me. I have grown and learned much from these encounters, and although too numerous to name, I am grateful to each of these special friends.

JENNI WOODHEAD: They say that one of the most important parts of the book, besides what it says inside, is the cover. I gave Jenni what I thought was a pretty good start. She sent back a piece of art that represented exactly how I felt about Africa. Thank you, Jenni, for all of the graphic work you did for my book. I love it and you are truly great at what you do.

BROOKE WARNER AND LINDA JOY MYERS, Ph.D.: Two of the people who gave me the resources to actually begin writing my memoir were Brooke Warner, the publisher of She Writes Press and Spark Press, and Linda Joy Myers, Ph.D. President and founder of National Association of Memoir Writers. Both women are multiple published authors and award winners and hold successful nationwide online workshops. It is through one of these workshops and weekend seminars I realized that through their coaching method, I could, in fact, accomplish this feat. I am truly grateful to you both, Brooke and Joy.

ANNALOU MENEKSEOGLU: Many thanks go to a very talented, delightful young woman, Annalou Menekseoglu. Anna is my tattoo artist. One day while I felt very far away from Africa, I got my first, and last, tattoo. It is a beautiful outline of Africa shaped into a woman's face. Anna is also the artist who drew the map of Nigeria in the front of this book. In addition to being a tattooist, she is a crafter and artist/illustrator originally from Chicago, and currently living in Tucker, Georgia. Thank you, Anna, for your beautiful work. I enjoyed working with you so much.

PHOTOGRAPHERS: I mustn't forget to thank the photograph contributors. Many were my personal pictures. I would like to thank the personal collection of the Craig's. They were the missionary couple that had much to do with the establishment of KA. Some pictures came from "The History of KA by Year." This was a most comprehensive work complete with a written history and class pictures as far back as 1945, when KA began. Some pictures were from the Sudan Interior Mission Archives, which includes pictures taken from many individuals within the mission with their permission. I am most appreciative of the use of these pictures.

About the Author

Cheryl King Duvall, PhD, is a psychologist degreed from Georgia State University in Atlanta, Georgia. She has over fourteen years' experience teaching at the undergraduate, graduate, executive, and online levels of education.

Specializing in organizational behavior, Cheryl has focused her research on designing organizations that will assure the success of human performance in the workplace. Along this line, Cheryl has published in seven peer-reviewed journals, one textbook case study, and seven papers which were used in peer-reviewed conference proceedings.

After graduation, Cheryl began consulting with Fortune 500 companies in organization design, and redesign; and she did both consulting and implementation of personnel selection and hiring systems. She focused on setting up organizational environments of "Assuring Individual Success" versus "Preventing Individual Failure" and how those two managerial values play out in day-to-day decision making.

When the flight attendants started calling her by her first name as she arrived on the plane, Cheryl realized she was probably doing too much traveling and consulting, so she started teaching at a private university in Atlanta and spending more time at home with her family. She became an associate professor of management and a department chair. After fifteen years of consulting followed by almost fourteen years of teaching, Cheryl retired from the corporate and teaching worlds to do what her heart had always wanted to do—work with children living with autism and other special needs.

Cheryl is an accomplished quilter and an avid hiker. She has climbed Mt. Whitney, the highest point in the continental US, and Mt. Chirripó, the highest point in Costa Rico. The next mountain on her list is Mt. Kilimanjaro, the highest point in Africa. She also wants to finish hiking the Appalachian Trail. She has currently hiked from Springer Mountain to the Smoky Mountains in North Carolina. She knows she could not have accomplished any of this without the encouragement and help of her loving and constant support team—her beloved husband of over forty years, two loving sons, her daughter-in-law, and two precious grandsons whom she adores.

Printed in Great
Britain
by Amazon

32112047R00120